A Simj

C000050842

The PC

L. Steven

Prentice Hall Europe

London New York Toronto Sydney Tokyo Singapore Madrid
Mexico City Munich Paris

First published in 1998 as Le PC – Se Former en 1 Jour by
Simon & Schuster Macmillan (France)
This edition published 1999 by
Prentice Hall Europe
An imprint of
Pearson Education Limited
Edinburgh Gate
Harlow
Essex CM20 2JE, England

© 1997 Simon & Schuster Macmillan (France)
19, rue Michel Le Comte
75003 Paris
France

Translated by Berlitz Translation Services UK, Baldock, Hertfordshire

Printed and bound in Great Britain by
Redwood Books, Trowbridge, Wiltshire

Library of Congress Cataloging-in-Publication Data

Available from the publisher

British Library Cataloguing in Publication Data

A catalogue record for this book is available from the British Library
ISBN 0-13-0212520-0

---

1 2 3 4 5 03 02 01 00 99

Table of Contents

Introduction

A PC THAT PUTS YOU AT EASE

The aim of this little book is essentially to make you familiar with the hardware environment of the computer. Everyone has heard of software programs, whether they are directly involved with computers or not. Everyone knows roughly how they work and what they are used for: they allow the user to increase his working power tenfold by making ultra-high-performance computational tools available to him. The hardware of the PC, however, involves technology and is not designed to put you at ease.

Designed clearly and simply, the "Teach Yourself In 1 Day" series will allow you, hour by hour, to study the ABC of the PC. There's no need to follow the lessons in order as each new chapter forms a unit in itself. After reading this book, you will master the common technical terms and therefore will be able to get the most out of your computer, whether at home or at work.

A PC THAT PRODUCES RESULTS

Once the technical aspects have been demystified, you are in a position to move on to achievements which are a little more professional, to go, for example, beyond simple letter writing or the conventional family budget calculation. If you equip yourself with peripherals, you can transform your computer into a photographic laboratory and perform touching up on screen. If you have children, your computer can be transformed into a video games base. You can install the latest CD-ROMs or maybe even design one yourself. It's not impossible. Just find yourself an editor and make a start!

A PC THAT BREAKS NEW GROUND

After reading this book, you will become one of the many Englishmen to have decided to get onto the Internet because you will have understood its advantages: exchanges with a correspondent from the other end of the world for the price of a local telephone call and access to instantaneous and exhaustive information. The Internet can also act as a dictionary, an encyclopedia, a records office, a video creation laboratory, the news, the weather forecast, etc.

A PC THAT IS PART OF YOUR LIFE

Now that you have your own special PC work station, you can be self-sufficient and independent and enjoy a new relationship with your colleagues, one which is more direct, more egalitarian, more immediate and more universal. Your PC will change your life. Without a doubt.

These notes provide additional information about the subject concerned.

These notes indicate a variety of shortcuts: keyboard shortcuts, 'wizard' options, techniques reserved for experts, etc.

These notes warn you of the risks associated with a particular action and, where necessary, show you how to avoid any pitfalls.

Hour 1

The central unit

THE CONTENTS FOR THIS HOUR

- A better life with your PC
- The case
- The power supply
- The ports
- The floppy disk drive
- The motherboard
- The microprocessor
- The bus

A BETTER LIFE WITH YOUR PC

You will be pleased to hear your PC is going to increase your potential. It will allow you to increase your productivity, reduce the amount of drudgery and improve quality in many areas.

If you are artistically minded, your PC will allow you to create original works, with many variants, all very easily. If you write well but make the odd spelling mistake, the spellchecker incorporated in your word processor will correct the faults for you. Finally, if you write illegibly, the handwritten character fonts will allow you to pass as an expert calligrapher.

Your PC is the ideal tool for managing your work more effectively.

Resistance ...

The most difficult thing is to make a start. It is generally the literary minded who need the most persuading. They worry that computers will turn them into cold technicians, unable to think for themselves.

To put their minds at rest, it will be nothing of the kind. Data processing, the Internet and multimedia are in no way incompatible with poetry, drawing, even meditation. Any form of art may even find an unsuspected medium there.

Go on, then, switch it on, don't be frightened!

Figure 1.1: Switched-on generation, don't hesitate any longer!

A piece of history

- 1900: Samuel Morse's telegraph, Graham Bell's telephone and Thomas Edison's dictation machine make their appearance.

- 1917: the company CTR becomes IBM (International Business Machines). IBM produces punched cards and typewriters.

- 1930: calculating machines are used in offices. A new professional breed makes its appearance: the programmer.

- 1936: Alan Turing's article on artificial intelligence "*Computing Machinery and Intelligence*" is published.

- 1941: the Nazi period, alas, contributes towards the development of the computer. The engineer Konrad Zuse creates the Z3.

- 1946: the ENIAC program, ancestor of the computer, appears. With its 20,000 valves, it performs the calculations necessary for producing the hydrogen bomb.

- 1950 to 1970: Robert Noyce creates the company Intel (Integrated Electronics), still number one in the processor market.

- 1975: the Altair computer is produced by the firm MITS.

- 1976: Steve Wozniak and Steve Jacobs create Apple I in Silicon Valley.

- 1981: IBM's personal computer is born.

- 1986: Bill Gates launches Microsoft Windows.

- 1989: Intel presents its new processor, the 80486.

- 1990: Windows 3.1 is created by Microsoft.

- 1991: IBM introduces its Multimedia PC.

- 1993: Microsoft launches Windows NT. Linda Steven is initiated into computing by her professor Jacques de Schryver, whom she thanks.

- 1994 to 1999: the Internet and multimedia make their way into homes.

Figure 1.2: No further without your PC!

What is a PC?

Your PC, or *Personal Computer*, is a very friendly assembly of plastic, metal and programs. The plastic and metal is the *hardware*. The programs are the *software*.

1. Hardware

2. Software: the programs

- The operating software: this organises the running of the various hardware aspects of the PC.

- The applications software: word processors, spreadsheets, graphics packages, etc.

- The utilities: software for standard operations such as copying, compression, recovery of lost data, reorganisation of the hard disk, formatting, etc.

The term PC is now commonly used for Personal Computer.

Figure 1.3: The hardware

Which PC should you choose?

In order to choose a PC wisely, it is necessary to consider all the items which will make up your future installation and what you wish to use them for: case, central unit, screen, CD-ROM drive, keyboard, hard disk, speakers, graphics card, audio card, modem, etc. This will be dealt with in greater detail in Hour 11.

The central unit

The central unit is the heart of the PC.

It is composed of the following items:

- The case
- The power supply
- The ports
- The floppy disk drive
- The motherboard

- The microprocessor
- The hard disk (see Hour 6)
- The slots
- The RAM memory
- The cache memory
- The bus
- The fan

Figure 1.4: The central unit

THE CASE

The case, like the screen, keyboard or mouse, forms part of what is called the hardware.

The case, which is generally made from metal, protects the components of the computer from various forms of interference and shocks. The large format case or tower allows easy access to the expansion cards.

The most practical cases are so-called "flip-flop" cases which open under simple pressure, like car bonnets.

There are vertical or horizontal cases. The choice depends simply on the way in which the user intends to organise his or her desktop.

Should you choose a desktop or tower?

If you want to share a computer with the family, it is better to choose a case in the form of a desktop. One of its advantages is to support your screen and raise it slightly so that it can be more comfortably viewed. Having said that, desktop-style cases have far less capacity than other models and are not, for example, suited to holding large disks (5").

For professional use, it is better to have a tower. Unlike horizontal desktop cases, towers are arranged vertically. This saves space, particularly since they can stand on the floor next to your desktop. There are three categories: miniature, medium and large. A large tower has room for a 3½" drive plus several high-capacity 5¼" disks. Cards can be added or components changed to make it even more accessible.

POWER SUPPLY

The On/Off switch is situated on the power supply unit.

Wires run from the power supply unit to a socket and to the motherboard.

The power supply unit converts the power from the 240-volt mains supply to the voltage necessary for the computer, which is from 8 to 12 volts. It must have a power of no less than 200 and no more than 230 watts.

The PC is sensitive to voltage surges. Power failures can cause you to lose some of your work. You are therefore recommended to add electrical protection in the form of an uninterruptible power supply.

The power supply unit may be multi-socket or single-socket. The multi-socket unit is more functional and in no way affects voltage regulation.

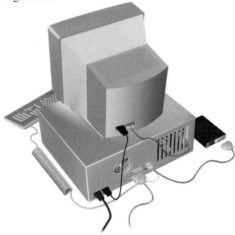

Figure 1.5: The central unit's power supply leads

Advice:

1. Unplug the computer in the event of a thunderstorm.

2. Do not plug your computer directly into an unearthed socket but rather into an inverter with short-circuit protection.

Figure 1.6: The central unit's power supply unit

THE PORTS

The central unit communicates with the outside world using ports:
one parallel port and two serial ports. Others can be added. For
example, the speaker peripheral has ports suited to its use.

- The parallel or LPT (*Line Printer*) ports: these send the data
  over eight separate cables, eight channels. They are fragile. The
  signal is attenuated beyond two or three metres. The parallel
  ports are mainly used to connect printers. The first printer is
  connected to LPT1, the second to LPT2, and so on.

- The serial ports: these send the data over one cable, one channel.
  They are slower than the parallel ports but more efficient over length.

- The SCSI port (pronounced "scuzzy"): this is designed to install
  several peripherals one behind the other, or cascaded. The SCSI
  ports transmit data at high speed. They are useful when the
  number of slots becomes insufficient.

- Other types of port: these are found, among other places, on
  the expansion cards, which are themselves plugged into the
  slots. These are destined to be replaced by USB connectors
  linked to the USB bus (see later).

Figure 1.7: Parallel port

Figure 1.8: Serial port

Figure 1.9: SCSI port

A port, whatever type it is, can be male or female, and is connected
to a cable of the opposite polarity.

*Figure 1.10: Impossible to confuse: a male connector and a
female connector!*

THE FLOPPY DISK DRIVE

The floppy disk drive allows information to be read from, written
to or stored on diskettes. A standard diskette can hold data equivalent
to the size of a 700-page book. It costs around 30 pence.

Figure 1.11: Floppy disk drives

There are two kinds of diskette:

- 3½"
- 5¼"

The diskette most commonly sold is the 3½". Most computers sold nowadays are equipped only with 3½" floppy disk drives.

If you want to use 5¼" diskettes, you can add a 5¼" floppy disk drive to your computer. However, this format is outdated.

The characteristics of the 3½" diskette are as follows:

- The 3½" Double Density (DD): 135 tpi — Capacity: 720 kbyte
- The 3½" High Density (HD): 135 tpi — Capacity: 1.44 Mbyte

tpi = tracks per inch
Mbyte = Megabytes = 1,024 kilobytes

A 3½" diskette has the following elements:

1. The retractable flap
2. The write window when the flap is pulled to the right
3. The write-protect tab
4. The filing label

Figure 1.12: 5¼" diskette

Figure 1.13: 5¼" floppy disk drive

Figure 1.14: 5¼" and 3½" diskettes

Figure 1.15: 3½" floppy disk drive

Figure 1.16: Write-protected diskettes

You must take certain precautions to protect your diskettes:

1. Avoid touching the exposed areas of the magnetic disk.

2. Store the diskette in a protective case.

3. Avoid placing the diskettes close to magnetic fields such as a television, motor or radio, or near magnetised metal objects.

4. File your diskettes vertically without putting anything on top.

5. Fill in the label before sticking it on the diskette. Writing with the diskette as a writing pad risks damaging it!

Formatting a diskette

Formatting a diskette is making it capable of being read and of receiving written information. So that the student can write correctly in his or her notebook, squares and lines are traced on blank pages. The squares and lines are the equivalent of the formatting of the diskette. The formatting divides the diskette into concentric tracks and into sectors. Unlike what happens on a record, which consists only of a single track, the tracks on disks are separated from one another. In the case of a conventional record, there is in reality only a single spiral, a single groove. In addition, each circle is divided into small sectors. In this way the information is fragmented into small blocks each having a precise address. So that the system can find its way around, it has a complete outline of the disk available. This is what is called the FAT or *File Allocation Table*.

How do you format a diskette?

1. Insert your diskette into the floppy disk drive.

2. Click on A:\ in the Windows File Manager.

3. Press the right button on the mouse.

4. Select the Format option from the context-sensitive menu you have just dropped down.

THE MOTHERBOARD

The motherboard is situated at the heart of the central unit. It is the main electronic system.

It is composed of the following items:

1. The central microprocessor, or CPU: this is the brain of the computer. It manages the information. Since 1998, this has been a Pentium 2 or equivalent, i.e. a very powerful processor capable of multimedia applications.

2. The RAM (*Random Access Memory*): this is arranged on DIMM or SIMM (*Dual/Single In-line Memory Module*) linear arrays which are plugged into the motherboard (see Hour 5).

3. The expansion slots, or connectors: you can plug additional electronic cards into these. The number of expansion slots depends on the size of your central unit.

4. The various pre-installed cards: controller card, screen card, etc.

5. The keyboard connectors.

6. The disk connectors.

7. The chips: these are integrated circuits which control the computer functions.

8. The linear arrays: the random access memory, or RAM, comes in the form of components soldered on to linear arrays.

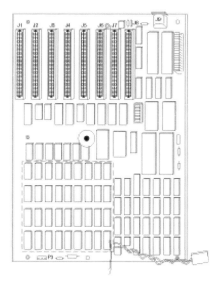

Figure 1.17: The motherboard

THE MICROPROCESSOR

The Intel 4004 was the very first microprocessor, invented by Ted Hoff in the years 1969 – 71 for Busicom, a Japanese client of Intel. Since Busicom had financial problems, the order was rejected. The 4004 was then put on sale in the classified advertisements on 15 November 1971, in the magazine *Electronic News*. The success was immediate. Computing had just entered a new era.

The microprocessor is the brain of the computer. It is an integrated circuit, a chip specialised in the management of information. It controls the flow of information and performs arithmetic operations, such as additions, or logical operations, such as comparisons. The microprocessor is so much the centre of the computer that the latter is often defined by the former. For example: a 386/33, a 486, a Pentium, Cyrix, AMD or Pentium II.

Figure 1.18: A microprocessor

The standard currently sold in the shops is a 32-bit Pentium II microprocessor. The bits in this case describe simultaneous inputs which the microprocessor data bus has.

A group of 8 bits constitutes what is called a byte, an octet, or a character.

The computer uses a binary notation system. Each character, number or symbol is coded into a group of 0s and 1s. Each 0 (off) or 1 (on) is equivalent to a *binary digit*, also called a *bit*.

To summarize:

1 bit = one binary position

1 byte = 1 character = 8 bits

1 kilobyte (kbyte) = 1,024 bytes

1 Megabyte (Mbyte) = 1,024 x 1,024 bytes

1 Gigabyte (Gbyte) = 1,024 x 1,024 x 1,024 bytes

The different kinds of microprocessor

- Intel 4004: the first and least powerful microprocessor

- 86: an abbreviation of the Intel 8086 chip number. This 16-bit processor can work, just like the 8088, only in 64-kbyte sections and with a total of 640 kbytes.

- 88: an abbreviation of the Intel 8088 chip number. This microprocessor allowed the use of all the software and peripherals designed for the Intel 8080 and the Zilog Z-80. IBM had chosen it for their first PC, but, being able to work only in 64-kbyte sections and with a total of 640 kbytes, it quickly imposed its limits on MS-DOS.

- 286: an abbreviation of the Intel 80286 chip number. The 286 is the 16-bit successor of the 8088 and 8086. This processor offered new performance for PCs.

- 386/33: an abbreviation of the Intel 80386 chip number. This microprocessor allows most of the software to be executed but has difficulty restoring the Windows 95 operating system correctly. The programs run very slowly.

- 486: an abbreviation of the Intel 80486 chip number. The PCs manufactured nowadays are almost all Pentiums, but there are still, and always will be, valiant 486s!

- Pentium 100 to 200: Pentiums are much more powerful than the old 486s. The MMX versions specialise in the processing of 3D multimedia applications and are ideal for running games.

- Pentium II (233 to 400 Mhz): Pentium IIs have been the norm since the first half of 1998. However, even at that time you would have been able to find versions that ran efficiently at 700 Mhz.

The bad news for anyone who has recently bought a computer is that things move very quickly. The good news is that, if you continue to wait, prices will continue to fall. A new piece of equipment will lose 40% of its value in its first year.

Pentium is the code name of the Intel 80586 component, also called the P5.

The most famous microprocessor manufacturers are:

- Intel Corporation: besides the microprocessors mentioned above, the creation of many other powerful components is owed to this company. They also market their own supercomputers.

- Motorola: the manufacturer of components including the famous 68000 series which have equipped the Macintosh, the Atari and the Amiga.

- National Semiconductor.

- AMD.

- CYRIX

  AMD and Cyrix manufacture quality components which are compatible with Intel and much less expensive.

Co-processors assist the processors for operations requiring many calculations. However, old co-processors have been integrated into the main component for some time now.

Computers have developed so much in the last few years that the main processor is now supported by ultra-powerful cards, particularly the famous 3DFX II graphics card.

"Co-processor" means an auxiliary microprocessor. It is the complement of the main microprocessor which performs the calculations. The co-processor plays an important role, particularly in graphics applications.

THE BUS

The bus is a system for transporting information. It resembles a motorway with several lanes connecting the microprocessor to the peripherals. The number of channels (bits) determines the quantity of information which can be carried at the same time. This also depends on the speed, i.e. the value in Mhz.

Buses have evolved in line with technology. The ISA bus appeared at the end of the 1970s. This was an eight-bit (eight-channel) bus with a speed of 8 Mhz. It was followed in the 1980s by the Microchannel bus and EISA (Enhanced ISA) bus, which had 32 channels (32 bits). Their speed has remained the same. The VLB (*Vesa Local Bus*), characterised by a speed of 40 Mhz and 32 channels, was brought out in 1992, followed two years later by the PCI bus. This had 64 channels (bits) and boasted a record transfer rate of 80 Mb per second. In 1998, the most popular bus was the USB or Universal Serial Bus. This first came out in 1995 and enables up to 127 peripherals to be connected to a PC without the use of multiple types of connector, without IRQ conflicts (i.e. interruptions), without address adjustment by means of jumpers and without DMA channel modifications.

New PCs automatically come (or at least should come) with a USB. It replaces Centronics, Mini-DIN and Sub-D parallel ports (ports for games, the printer, keyboard and mouse, modem and network adapter), and will soon replace those which have until now resisted. Thanks to the USB, a peripheral can be connected while the computer is switched on, thus allowing it to be recognised. This technique is known as "hot swapping".

Finally, there is the AGP (*Accelerated Graphics Port*) bus. This has cards fitted with the excellent 440LX graphics circuit (or equivalent). Brought out at the end of 1997, the AGP bus is a specialised bus which transports graphics data between the graphics card, the RAM and the processor. It has a transfer rate of 528 Mb per second and is perfectly suited for the processing of 3D graphics.

It should be said that the USB and AGP buses complement each other rather than the other way round. They run better under Windows 98. The latter is therefore strongly recommended.

Ports USB

Figure 1.23: USB technology allows you to add a peripheral without switching off your computer

Hour 2

The screen

THE CONTENTS FOR THIS HOUR

- The basic ideas
- Definition
- Resolution
- Colour
- The graphics card
- Configuring the graphics card and display

The screen is without doubt the most important item of comfort in your computer equipment. It displays all the information you enter, it is the screen you look at for several hours a day, and your well-being depends on its quality. From the 2CV to the Rolls, everyone can choose, and then progress.

THE BASIC IDEAS

In order to understand properly how a screen works, let us see what items it comprises.

The monitor can be monochrome or colour:

- Monochrome monitors display two colours: black and white, or black and green, or even black and yellow (amber). They are now rare.

- Colour monitors display between 16 colours and 16.7 million colours.

The monitor is composed of the following elements:

- Screen
- On/Off switch
- Brightness control knob
- Contrast control knob
- Vertical shift knob
- Horizontal shift knob
- Vertical size knob
- Horizontal size knob
- Frequency view knob
- Degaus button
- Stand

The most widely used start-of-the-range screen is a 14" colour screen with a definition of 800 × 600. This means that its diagonal measures 35 or 37.5 cm, its height is 600 pixels (dots) and its width 800 pixels. For a reasonable extra cost, a 17" screen, affording much greater comfort, can be obtained. Finally, the drop in prices makes some 19" screens affordable at £700, while it is even possible to find 21" screens, that is with a diagonal measuring 53 cm, for less than £900.

Figure 2.1: The monitor

The screen size

Given that the distance between the user and his or her screen will remain constant once installation is complete, two parameters must be taken into account with regard to readability.

- The distance from the eye to the screen

- The size of the screen itself

On a 14" screen, the most suitable display is 640 × 480.

On a 15" screen, a change to a 600 × 800 display is possible. For those who use a lot of graphics, a 17" screen will allow acceptable conditions of comfort with a 1024 × 768 display.

Why these strange figures? In the last case, it is simply a ratio of 4/3, since these are multiples of 256.

It is highly probable that all screens will soon change to the 16/9 format in order to become compliant with the standards for the television of the future.

The screen dot size

Although the screen diagonal is measured in inches, each equal to 2.54 cm, the accuracy of the screen is measured using *pitch*.

The pitch defines the distance which separates the left extremity of one dot from the left extremity of the next dot.

- A standard pitch corresponds to 0.28 mm.

- A high-quality pitch corresponds to 0.25 or 0.24 mm.

- An exceptional pitch corresponds to 0.21 mm.

The difference in cost between good quality and excellent quality is often very large.

This reference dot, called a *pixel*, is itself made up of three smaller dots, each corresponding to one of the three components, red, green and blue, which allow colour to be defined.

These dots define the standard dot. They therefore correspond to three photophores: one red, one green, and one blue, that is, inside the screen, they correspond to coatings sensitive to one colour and one only. Each dot of colour is defined by the closeness of these three fundamental dots. When the screen's electron gun selectively scans a precise photophore, this lights up in the colour to which it corresponds.

By means of the electronics, the scanning is performed many times a second. In this way the whole screen is refreshed, from 50 to 120 times a second depending on its quality.

Image stability

Perhaps you have observed that some screens seem to flicker when looked at from some distance, or are crossed by horizontal bands as can be seen in the cinema or on television. This phenomenon corresponds to the gap which exists between our perception and reality. An image perceived by the eye benefits from a phenomenon called *remanence*: the cells of the eye retain the image for longer than it actually lasts. This explains why we see the cinema and television images as a continuous movement and not as a series of fixed images.

Animals perceive things differently, often more quickly. That's why cats are not, as we are, fascinated by television.

The refresh rate, or the number of times a screen is redisplayed each second, defines how comfortable it is to use.

As the speed is insufficient in lower-end-of-the-range hardware, each scan redraws only every other line. It is known as *interlacing*. If you have the choice, however, you should choose a non-interlaced screen, that is a screen in which all the lines are refreshed simultaneously.

To summarize, a good screen must be non-interlaced and, secondly, must have a refresh rate of at least 75 Hertz.

Such screens are common today.

Also keep an eye on the capabilities offered for varying the screen definition, that is its number of dots in width and height, during use. This is because the scanning speed is a function of the number of dots to be dealt with. When the definition is increased, for example, from 640×480 to 600×800, the scanning speed is reduced since the system has to deal with a different number of dots.

When the appropriate software is not installed, this abrupt discontinuity in display, which occurs mainly when you change from a Windows application to a game in DOS mode, or vice versa, is accompanied by noise on the screen which can have serious drawbacks, in particular that of damaging the screen because of certain components which have overheated.

Certain pirating techniques consist of artificially forcing the screen to frequencies which are too high, in order to make the components heat up, and cause a failure. Therefore try not to leave a screen in this state for too long. If it lasts for more than a few seconds, switch off the screen, then the machine. Certain well-known brands of screen automatically put themselves in screensaver mode when they detect this phenomenon. This control equipment is frequent on 17" screens.

Screen adjustment

Let us now look at the hardware and physical means you have for adjusting the screen. The monitor has knobs which allow you to adjust:

- The contrast
- The brightness
- The vertical position
- The horizontal position

When your screen remains dark, although it is clearly on, the odds are that you have inadvertently disturbed the knobs controlling the contrast and brightness. Either that or the screensaver is on. In this case, all you need to do is lightly touch the mouse to return to the screen.

Figure 2.2: The monitor control knobs

DEFINITION

Definition describes the size of a screen or image as a number of dots.

A 600 × 800 screen has 480,000 dots. A 640 × 480 screen has 307,200 dots, that is, two thirds less. It can be seen therefore that an apparently modest change in the definition causes the display of far more information. It is therefore better to avoid scrolling the image too frequently, which you can achieve by choosing a higher definition. For maximum comfort, choose a definition of 1,024 × 768.

RESOLUTION

Resolution concerns the density of dots for a given measurement. It is measured in dots per inch, that is the number of pixels which can be put in line over a length of 2.54 cm.

Whereas definition measures the number of pixels which can be displayed on a screen, resolution measures the quality of the image. This will become greater as each square inch contains more and more dots.

Resolution is essential to quality. Let us leave the screen for a moment to examine the effect of printing resolution on reading a printout. A start-of-the-range laser printer uses a resolution of 300 dots per inch, which is generally satisfactory. It is necessary to be aware that, for a printer with a resolution of 600 dpi, the cost of the ink becomes prohibitive. Therefore be aware that, although the prices of the most advanced machines have dropped a great deal, this is not the case for the ink. You would get a bargain as regards the printer, but you would bankrupt yourself with the ink ...

Colour

Some screens claim to display 16.7 million colours! How is such a phenomenon possible? Let us clarify first of all that very few users are capable of telling the difference between so many colours.

How can so many different colours be created and why?

A colour is defined by 3 characteristics:

- Its hue.

- Its brightness, or intensity.

- Its saturation, which defines the way in which it differs from white.

This last idea requires an explanation and a minimum amount of knowledge on the working of the eye. The human eye is equipped with three pigments sensitive to, respectively, red, green and blue, which are known as the *primary colours*.

In reality there are other primary colours which are defined as a set of four colours that, according to how they are combined, can be used to create new ones. It is for this reason that, in printing, the system is known as subtractive; its basic colours are respectively:

- Yellow: red + green in an additive system, or white – blue in a subtractive system.

- Cyan: green + blue in an additive system, or white – red in a subtractive system.

- Magenta: red + blue in an additive system, or white – green in a subtractive system.

- Black: an absence of colours in an additive system, or magenta + yellow + cyan in a subtractive system, that is a total absorption of colours.

The screen works in additive mode, that is by superimposing the colours by projecting electrons onto the photophores. The printing system is known as subtractive since the paper absorbs the colours and reflects only those which are able to bounce off. An ink therefore defines the colours through those which it absorbs. For example, a blue ink absorbs all colours except blue. Remember that black is the absence of colour, or is obtained when all the colours are absorbed. White results from the simultaneous presence of all the colours, to the point that none of them in particular can be distinguished any more. A white ink is therefore an ink which does not absorb any colour.

This is why a white page lit by a red light seems red, while a black page under the same conditions remains black. In the first case the red light bounces off; in the second, if the ink is of good quality, it is absorbed.

THE GRAPHICS CARD

Once you've got these ideas in your head, you can choose a screen and a graphics card. The latter forms an essential addition to a high-quality screen. This is because the 16.7 million colours are obtained by irregular variations caused by the intensity of the electrons.

The more numerous the colours, the more space their coding takes. A 256-colour dot uses one byte, a 65,536-colour dot requires two of them, and a 16.7 million-colour dot uses three bytes.

The transfer of information is proportional to its size. A high-quality screen, that is one with a high definition and a large number of colours, will need to make use of a graphics card which has high-speed components for processing, storing and reconstructing the image.

Therefore there are specialised cards for the display of two- or three-dimensional games.

Others allow results close to the cinema or television. Others again, the most developed, allow the acquisition of images in real time from an external source, camera, camcorder, video recorder or television.

At the top of the range, the best type of 3D card for the Pentium II 1998 seems to be the 3DFX II. This specialises in the processing of 3D images, which it processes and displays very quickly. It uses the Voodoo 2 circuit and should preferably have 8 Mb of RAM. Numerous manufacturers offer 3DFX II cards. They generally cost less than £170.

Prices

Prices vary from £25 for start-of-the-range cards to almost £1,000 for video cards. A good graphics card can reasonably cost between 10% and 20% of the total price of the configuration. This is because it constitutes on its own a veritable small processing plant with its own high-speed memory unit for transferring the image directly to the screen – and without going through the computer bus.

Today, under Windows 95, with a 1,024 × 768 screen, a memory of 4 to 12 Mbytes often has to be used on its graphics card.

The difference will be obvious to those who often switch from one Internet session to another, or from one program to another. With 1 Mbyte of graphics memory, the display may take several seconds. With 4 or more Mbytes, it is instantaneous.

CONFIGURING THE GRAPHICS CARD AND DISPLAY

To configure the graphics card with Windows 95 or 98, you must go through several relatively simple steps.

As a rule, the monitor and video card form part of the basic configuration when you purchase your computer.

1. Click on the Start menu.

2. Select Settings.

3. Click on Control Panel and confirm.

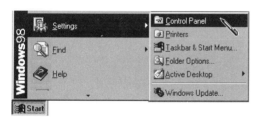

Figure 2.3: Install your graphics card using the Hardware Installation Wizard

4. Double-click on the Add New Hardware icon. If you have Plug and Play hardware, Windows will probably have already detected it. In this case, the following steps can be skipped. Otherwise, launch the automatic search option. If Windows does not detect your card, you will have to install it manually. If Windows finds nothing new, this may mean that the hardware is already installed. To check and/or modify, click on Next.

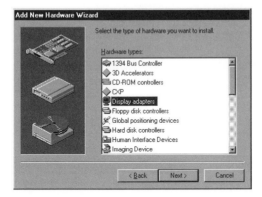

Figure 2.4: Install your graphics card using the Add New Hardware Wizard

5. In the ideal case, Windows will recognise your hardware straight away. Otherwise, select the type of hardware you want to install, a graphics card in this case.

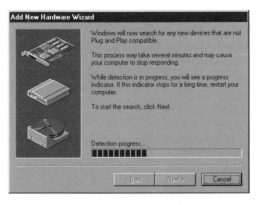

Figure 2.5: Detection of the graphics card

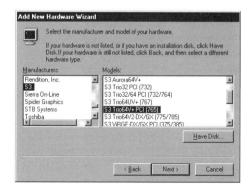

Figure 2.6: Windows 98 has the documentation of the main manufacturers. The chances are your card will be contained in this documentation

6. Click on the manufacturer and model of your hardware.

7. Click Next to have your driver installed from Windows 95 or click Have Disk to install your driver from a floppy disk.

8. Insert the installation disk (or CD ROM) for your video card.

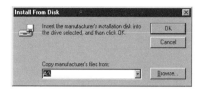

Figure 2.7: The Install from Disk dialog box enables you to install your video card

Once your graphics card is installed, you will be able to adjust the display settings for your screen.

1. Click on the Start menu.

2. Select Settings.

3. Click on Control Panel.

4. Double-click on the Display icon.

5. Click on the Settings tab. Choose your settings. For example, 65,536 (16 bits) colours using 1,024 × 768.

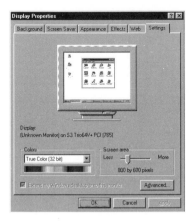

Figure 2.8: The Settings tab of the Display Properties dialog box enables you to set parameters such as the screen definition and the number of colours

Hour 3

Mice and keyboards

THE CONTENTS FOR THIS HOUR

- The conventional keyboard
- The ergonomic keyboard
- The mouse
- The trackball
- The trackpoint
- The trackpad
- The joystick or game pad
- Equipment for disabled people

The keyboard is an input peripheral. You can fit different kinds of them on to your computer. A keyboard must have alphabetic keys, numeric keys and function keys. The layout of the keys varies according to country.

The main keyboard type is:

- The QWERTY keyboard: the American keyboard

THE CONVENTIONAL KEYBOARD

The conventional keyboard is provided with keys with a layout similar to that of old typewriters.

- The alphanumeric keys or typing keys, which allow letters and figures to be entered.

- The function keys F1 to F12.

- The cursor movement keys, which allow movement within the text.

- The numeric keys on the keypad, which allow writing of figures and movements within the text.

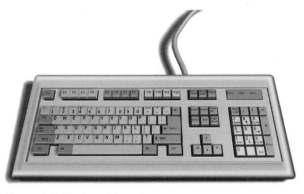

Figure 3.1: Keyboard layout

THE ERGONOMIC KEYBOARD

The ergonomic keyboard has a key spacing different from that of the conventional keyboard; certain keys, in particular Ctrl, Alt, Alt Gr, and possibly the Enter key, are larger and more practical. The keyboard is divided into three or four blocks by a space of irregular form, bevelled or triangular, the purpose of which is to space out the keys so that they are more suited to the position of the hands.

Some keyboards broaden this principle with extending guides. A keyboard of variable size is then obtained, which can be adapted to the build and posture of the user.

One category of keyboard, not as common, incorporates infrared radiation which allows communication with the computer without any lead connection. In this way, you can work with your feet up in complete bliss.

Some keyboards have additional keys, which is the case with the Microsoft keyboard. Between the Ctrl and Alt keys, a key bearing the Windows icon gives access to the Start menu.

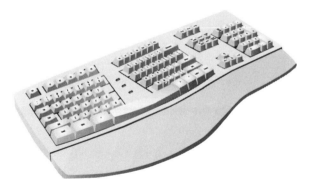

Figure 3.2: The ergonomic keyboard

Configuring the keyboard

Do you want to configure your keyboard, e.g. by adding a language? Here is how to access the Control Panel for the keyboard.

1. Click on the Start menu.

2. Select Settings.

3. Click on Control Panel.

4. Double-click on the Keyboard icon.

Figure 3.3: Click on the Keyboard option in the Control Panel

Once the Keyboard icon is selected, a dialog box opens, composed of three tabs:

- Speed: makes it possible to set parameters such as Cursor Blink or Character Repetition frequency.

- Language: makes it possible to add a language from the fifty offered in the drop-down list.

- General: gives information concerning the keyboard type

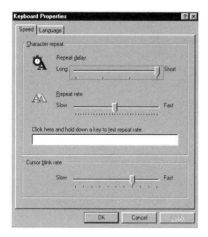

Figure 3.4: The Keyboard Properties dialog box

To add a language:

1. Click on the Start menu.

2. Select Settings.

3. Click on Control Panel.

4. Double-click on the Keyboard icon.

5. Select the Language tab of the Keyboard Properties dialog box.

6. Click on the Add command button.

7. Select your chosen language in the Add Language dialog box.

8. Activate the indicator on the Taskbar once the language has been selected.

9. Once your various languages are installed and the Activate Indicator on Taskbar box has been ticked, an indicator showing the default language appears in the Windows Taskbar. To change from one language to another, click on this indicator, then on the language you want to use.

It is up to you to define the shortcut keys for changing from one language to another during typing. To do this, go to the Switch Between Languages area positioned under the Language tab.

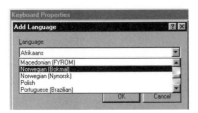

Figure 3.5: The Add Language dialog box

Keyboard maintenance

Of all the items which make up your computer installation, the keyboard is by far the most exposed to dust and dirt. This is all the more true if there are several of you in the family using it. You would be surprised the different sources of dirt which fall between the keys of your keyboard. Hair, sweet and savoury crumbs, dust, paper, etc.

All these small scraps end up sooner or later jamming the keyboard mechanism.

Provide yourself with cotton buds, a glass cleaner and tweezers.

1. Lightly spray your keyboard with glass cleaner.

2. Pass the cotton bud between the keys.

3. Using the tweezers, dismantle the keys which are especially dirty.

4. Blow on the keyboard to remove the largest areas of dust.

THE MOUSE

The mouse has become, with time and the use of data processing, an extension of the hand. The mouse is a fundamental intermediary between the computer and the hand, in the hollow of which it fits perfectly.

Designed and perfected by Douglas Engelbart and Bill English in 1963, the mouse was improved by Xerox in 1970. It was popularised by Apple at the beginning of the 1980s. But it was the PC that made it universal with the arrival of Windows. When it was designed, it was only as part of an ambitious project aimed at "improving human intelligence". As its inventor said during a famous interview: "At the time, I had been working for twelve years on different ways of helping people increase their capacity for solving complex problems. We had envisaged getting them to work on problem-solving programs on work stations. This assumed that it was possible for them to interact with the displayed information by using an accessory capable of moving the cursor on screen. Several solutions already existed such as graphic pens and joysticks, etc.".

In order to carry out his tests, Engelbart managed to secure the support of NASA. While the mouse did better than the trackball and joystick, it lost out by a whisker to another accessory which was even faster and knee-operated! The mouse also suffered from another crippling fault: without gravity, it floated in space.

In the end, Engelbart perfected the prototype of the mouse with the help of his collaborator Bill English. It was very simple, with two wheels for drawing straight vertical and horizontal lines. It was not possible to move directly in a diagonal direction.

That, then, is how the mouse was born, in the laboratories of the Stanford Research Institute, with the unexpected help of NASA. Since then, it has enjoyed three decades of development. Its technology as well as its appearance has been considerably improved. In everyday life, it has replaced the pen, felt pen and pencil. An extension of the hand, it has become an established feature of the western world.

Figure 3.6: Douglas Engelbart and the first mouse, assembled by Bill English

Figure 3.7: Three models of mouse

There are different kinds of mouse. The quality of a mouse lies in its sensitivity, its resolution, its movement and the number of buttons it has (two or three). Its precision must be excellent.

The standard Microsoft mouse offers two buttons while some software programs require three.

Figure 3.8: The mouse

Configuring the mouse

To modify the double-click speed:

1. Click on the Start menu.
2. Select Settings.
3. Click on Control Panel.
4. Double-click on the Mouse icon.
5. Select the Buttons tab.
6. Set the speed.

There are four different types of tab on the Mouse Properties dialog box.

- Buttons: enables the button configuration and the double-click speed to be set.
- Pointers: enables a pointer model to be chosen.
- Motion: enables the pointer speed and the pointer trails to be set.
- General: specifies the type of mouse connected to the computer

Figure 3.9: The Mouse Properties dialog box.

How does the mouse work?

There is a "mouse" language, which is the language of all micro initiates. Let us review the terms which recur most often for defining the work carried out using the mouse:

- Slide the mouse over the text.
- Double-click on a word.
- Click on an object.
- Move a pointer.
- Hold a key down.
- Release the button.

Mouse mat

Careful! No mouse should be without its mat. The mouse mat, a piece of, usually, rectangular-shaped rubber, makes it possible to cushion the jolts given to the mouse during movements. Without a mat, the mice deteriorate quickly. Mouse mats cost from £1 to £2 each, sometimes less, and exhibit a great variety of colours and designs – an economical way of making your work space friendlier and more attractive!

Figure 3.10: Mouse mats to make your computer sing!

IntelliMouse

IntelliMouse is the new Microsoft mouse. It is provided with a small wheel situated between the left and right buttons. On turning this small wheel, the document scrolls on the screen very quickly.

The Microsoft IntelliMouse software makes it possible to carry out a greater number of manoeuvres from the mouse. It gives you the capability, for example, of scrolling and zooming directly from the mouse. To zoom with IntelliMouse, hold down the Ctrl key on the keyboard while turning the wheel.

For scrolling using IntelliMouse, you must move the insertion point before making any modification. To do this you just need to click at the place where you want to intervene in the movement.

The IntelliMouse mouse allows you, among other things, to:

- Scroll a number of lines upward or downward in a single go: turn the wheel forwards or backwards.

- Zoom in or out: hold the Ctrl key down while turning the wheel forwards or backwards.

- Enlarge or reduce the titles in Drawing mode: click on a title, then hold down the SHIFT key while turning the wheel forwards or backwards.

▬▬▬ Maintaining the mouse

The mouse is the input peripheral most used after the keyboard. It is therefore, like the latter, particularly exposed to wear and various types of dirt. The slightest clogging of the mouse affects the accuracy of the cursor. How should you clean your mouse?

1. Undo the cover situated under the mouse.

2. Take out the ball.

3. Wipe it with a cloth.

4. Remove the dust from the case by blowing over it.

5. Loosen the dust encrusted on the roller rings with tweezers and with the help of a cotton bud.

THE TRACKBALL

The trackball, trackpoint and trackpad are offshoots of the mouse. They are well known to users of laptops.

Figure 3.11: The laptop and its trackball

The trackball is a ball rolling in a support equipped with sensors and designed to replace the mouse.

It can be compared to a mouse placed on its back.

The user no longer needs to move the ball but rather turn it using a thumb.

THE TRACKPOINT

The trackpoint resembles a lozenge, a point situated in the middle of the laptop's keyboard, between the letters B, H and G. It is equipped with four potentiometers which enable it to be tilted in different directions depending on the pressure of your finger.

THE TRACKPAD

The trackpad is the most delicate of the Track cousins. It is a small rectangle marked out in squares with a smooth surface situated in front of the laptop's keyboard. It records the movements made by the finger. A simple light touch is sufficient. It combines transmission speed and sensitivity.

THE JOYSTICK OR GAME PAD

The joystick or game pad is used with 3D games and is connected to a games port on the central unit.

There are two kinds of joystick:

- A flat game pad with control buttons.
- A conventional joystick with control buttons.

Figure 3.12: An indispensable entertainment accessory

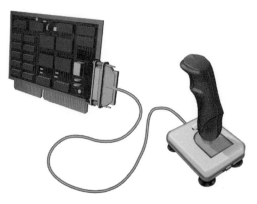

Figure 3.13: The joystick connected to its games port

Configuring the joystick

To install your joystick, you need to carry out the following operations:

1. Click on the Start menu.

2. Select Settings.

3. Click on Control Panel.

4. Double-click on the Joystick icon.

5. Select the Joystick tab.

Figure 3.14: The Joystick Properties dialog box under the Joystick Configuration tab

EQUIPMENT FOR DISABLED PEOPLE

As a complement to the conventional keyboard, there are a number of accessories designed for people with hand disabilities and even for tetraplegics. There are, for example, keyboards with keys which are designed to receive the pressure of a pencil, without sliding towards other keys. It is possible to activate this type of keyboard by head movements whilst holding the pencil in the mouth. Each

key has the shape of a small crater. A helmet fitted with an *eye-tracker* has a system which analyses the movements of the eye and the time the focus of the eye remains fixed on a precise area.

Originally, this helmet was designed for jet aircraft pilots who could in this way communicate with their on-board computer without using their hands.

Today it enables paraplegics and tetraplegics to carry out, by means of a series of simple conventions, using eye movements, actions which in an able-bodied person correspond to movements and clicks of the mouse.

Hour 4

Printers

THE CONTENTS FOR THIS HOUR

- The different types of printer
- Choosing a printer
- Installing a printer under Windows 98 or 95
- Configuring the printer
- Minor problems and their solutions

THE DIFFERENT TYPES OF PRINTER

The printer is an output peripheral. There are four main categories of printer:

- Dot matrix printer: the head of this printer is composed of a matrix of metal pins which strike the paper through a ribbon.

The quality of this printer depends on the number of pins which make up the head and which strike like hammers under an electromagnetic field. There are heads with 9, 18, 24 and 48 pins. The dot matrix printer, the printer used by microcomputers in the 1980s, is less used today. The print speed varies from 80 to 300 characters per second.

- Inkjet printer: the printing of characters is performed using minute jets of ink from hollow pins known as nozzles. The print speed varies from 70 to 300 characters per second.

- Daisy-wheel printer: this owes its name to the little flower-like wheel which contains the characters. The print system is that of the typewriter. Each character is written by the striking of a small (petal-like) hammer on the daisy wheel. The print speed varies from 15 to 60 characters per second. This is obviously very slow. Another major drawback is that, beyond a certain speed, vibrations occur and reduce the print quality.

- Laser printer: this uses the same process as the photocopier, namely the electrostatic or xerographic process. It replaces the original document with a laser beam. The print speed varies between 4 and 20 pages per minute (or more) depending on the printer.

Figure 4.1: A laser printer

Figure 4.2: A dot matrix printer

If it were not for marketing decisions, all laser printers could simultaneously be used as photocopiers, fax machines, scanners and modems. They all use the same principle of scanning a document with a laser beam in order to reproduce it.

CHOOSING A PRINTER

Your choice of printer should be determined both by the type of work you wish to carry out and by the quality and speed of the print rendition required.

- Resolution: the quality of a printer is measured in dots per inch. Conventional printers print in 300 dpi. Increasingly, manufacturers are offering machines with a resolution of 600 dpi, at low prices.

600 dpi black and white printers, often very cheap to buy, prove to be quite costly to run. This is because the special ink suitable for this resolution is between 40% and 200% more expensive. Consider asking the sales person the price of the ink and if there is any currently in stock. In a good many cases, the reply to these two questions is 'No'. Express

surprise at the price difference between this and other ink and you may be told that it is because twice as much ink is necessary, which is not true, for two reasons. The first is that, when the resolution doubles, the number of dots per square inch is multiplied by four (since we are talking about a surface area). Next, although the number of dots increases, this is because they are smaller. The amount of ink necessary remains exactly the same.

- Print speed: the print speed is measured in number of characters per second (cps) or pages per minute.

- Strike quality: daisy-wheel printers are slower than dot matrix printers but offer a 'letter' strike quality. It is laser printers that offer the highest quality of characters with the widest variety of fonts.

- Paper format: paper format and type of drive are also important. The pin feed system requires the exclusive use of listing paper. The other printers are equipped with a single-sheet-feed system.

- Noise nuisance: dot matrix printers and daisy-wheel printers are the noisiest. They require the use of an insulating hood. Inkjet printers and laser printers are quiet.

The laser printer has become the standard for microcomputers.

Advice:

- For printing only black and white text, all printers are acceptable.

- For printing black and white drawings and graphics, laser printers give a more satisfactory rendition than do inkjet printers. The line of the drawings is finer.

- For printing colour, the inkjet offers a good quality/price ratio. The colour laser printer is, sadly, still beyond the reach of most personal budgets (around £3,000).

Some printers are delivered with few character fonts. To increase your stock of character fonts, you must buy fonts which can be downloaded from the software or install cartridges on the printer. However, the simple solution is to use the fonts which come supplied with Windows.

INSTALLING A PRINTER UNDER WINDOWS 98 OR 95

To install a printer under Windows 98 or 95, proceed as follows:

1. Click on Start.
2. Select Settings.
3. Click on Printers.
4. Click on Add Printer.

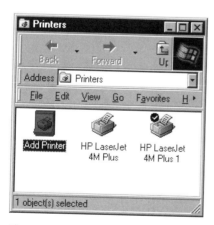

Figure 4.3: The first step is to click on the Add Printer icon

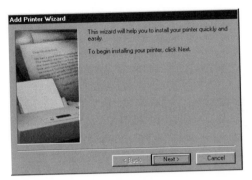

Figure 4.4: Identical under Windows 98 and 95 (with the exception of the image on the left), the Add Printer Wizard guides you throughout the installation of your new printer

5. Select the name of the manufacturer of your printer.

6. Click on the name of the printer you want to install.

7. Click on the Have disk command button if the driver is delivered with the printer.

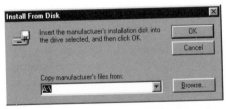

Figure 4.5: The Install from Disk dialog box

8. Click on the Next button to configure the port.

9. Configure the port. You have two ports. The one assigned to a single printer is LPT1. Tick the Check port state before printing box.

The port is a serial or parallel output or may be of some other type, particularly where telecommunications are concerned. The serial port comes in the form of a plug (connector). As a rule your computer is likely to be equipped with two parallel ports.

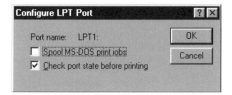

Figure 4.6: Configure LPT Port dialog box

CONFIGURING THE PRINTER

The print a document under Windows 95, the procedure is simple. Carry out the following operations in succession:

1. Open the File menu.

2. Click on the Print option.

3. Choose the settings you require.

4. Click on the Properties command button which gives you access to the Properties dialog box for your printer. For example: print odd and even pages, print odd pages only, number of copies, include automatic insertions when printing, etc.

The properties of your printer

1. Open the File menu.

2. Click on the Print option.

3. Select the Properties command button. The Properties dialog box for your printer appears on the screen with its four tabs.

Figure 4.7: The Properties dialog box for your printer

The four tabs of the Properties dialog box for the printer are as follows:

- **Paper**: sets the paper size (US letter, A4, executive, US legal, etc.), envelopes, paper orientation (portrait, that is vertical, or landscape, that is horizontal), its source (upper tray, manual feed, manual envelope feed).

- **Graphics**: sets the resolution (75, 150 or 300 dpi), rastering (coarse or fine grain) and intensity (light to dark on a scale of 0 to 200).

- **Fonts**: allows downloading and printing of TrueType fonts.

- **Device options**: makes it possible to set the way in which the driver manages the use of the printer's memory.

INSTALLING A SECOND PRINTER

Installing a second printer is not difficult and has become increasingly more common. People who already own a black and white printer are tempted by colour inkjet printers because they have become cheaper. What should you do?

First of all, it is important to realise that some printers are installed using a serial port and some using a parallel port. A port is just an input/output connection. All you need to do is look at the back of your computer to know which one is available. In the rare event that all the ports are in use, you should reckon on paying between £10 and £20 to install a Com 3 or 4 port. If this means nothing to you or fills you with a slight feeling of apprehension, ask a more experienced friend for help. Either that or consult a specialist – but be prepared to pay!

Once you have connected your printer, install its software in exactly the same way as you did for your first printer. The different ways in which you use them will depend on what you want to use them for. For example, if you use your computer mainly for word-processing, the black and white printer will be defined as the default setting. However, if you decide you want to use your computer to create your own headed paper or logo, you will probably want to use you new colour printer to make the most of your colours.

At this point, rather than clicking on the print icon on the toolbar in order to print, open the File menu and click on the print option. In the dialog box, you have to redefine your choice of printer. To do this, proceed as follows:

1. Go to the text field at the top of the print dialog box.

2. Click on the small arrow to the right of the name of the active printer. A drop-down list appears containing all the installed printers.

3. Click on the printer you want. It is easy to switch from one to another.

Now print by specifying the parameters. Colour printers have many different options which need to be properly understood, such as paper category, print quality, adjustment and many other details. Depending on the options you choose, the printing time can be fast (in draft mode) to rather slow (for high-quality printouts). You therefore have to ask yourself whether it is worth having a colour printer if it deprives you of the best quality.

You now know how to get the best of both worlds by quickly switching from one printer to another.

THE COLOUR PRINTER

You have an urgent document to output and your printer lets you down. Nothing is more annoying. Below is a list of printing difficulties and their solutions.

- **Your printer prints several sheets at the same time**. This may be due to the quality of the paper itself. It may be too thin, for example, or packed too tightly. Before filling your printer's feeder, don't forget to fan your paper properly.

- **Your sheets come out crooked**. Make sure that the guides arranged either side of your paper feed tray grip your sheets properly.

- **The printer indicates 'Paper out' yet the tray is full of paper**. Check that your tray is fully inserted, up to the end stop.

- **The sheets are not being inserted automatically**. You have to insert them manually.

  The paper is driven by rollers. These may be covered in dust. If they are, clean them using a vacuum cleaner with a very fine nozzle. Cotton buds and glass cleaner are also very useful, as is an aerosol ink cleaner. This dissolves traces of ink on any printing hardware such as paper drive drums, rollers, bearings, rubber characters, etc.

- **The printer doesn't print, there is no power and the lights are off**. There's probably nothing to worry about. You may have forgotten to plug your printer in. Check that the cable is correctly connected to your computer and that the adaptor is properly plugged into the mains.

- **The colour of the ink is very faint and practically unreadable**. The toner cartridge in your laser printer is nearly empty and should be replaced.

The toner is an electrostatic ink used for photocopiers and laser printers. Its fineness allows a greater or lesser degree of resolution.

Fleabag!

Figure 4.7: An example of printing

The corona wire is a metal wire mesh which plays a part in the magnetisation of the drum and therefore in the positioning of the ink. Make sure that it does not get clogged up with dust.

Hour 5

The memory

THE CONTENTS FOR THIS HOUR

- The memory
- The central memory, or random access memory (RAM)
- Read-only memory (ROM)
- Cache memory
- The motherboard

The memory is one of the items which defines how comfortable a computer is to use as well as its power. It would be more exact to say that it allows the available power to express itself. A top-of-the-range Pentium II requires a random access memory (RAM) of between 32 and 64 Mb. However, this amount will doubtless soon be exceeded.

THE MEMORY

If there is one area in which you might well get lost, it is without doubt the memory. Many terms are in use to describe different areas of computer memory and sometimes different manufacturers use different terms to describe the same thing. Without some idea of what each term refers to it is easy to become very confused when making choices over the purchase of memory.

These are some of the terms you may hear:

- **Linear arrays**: name of the 4, 8 or 16, 32 or even 64 Mb memory block which plugs into the motherboard.

- **Disk cache**: area reserved for dynamic data exchanges.

- **60-nanosecond (ns) memory**: normal standard memory that can be found on SIMM EDO linear arrays. The default memory is between 70 and 80 ns.

- **10-nanosecond (ns) memory**: rapid standard memory that can be found on DIMM SDRAM linear arrays.

 A nanosecond is one thousand millionth of a second.

- **Bubble memory**: a once promising technology.

- **Cache memory**: intermediate storage memory.

- **First-level cache memory**: cache located on the processor itself and known as the main cache memory.

- **Second-level cache memory**: area of memory located in the immediate vicinity of the processor. It stores the most recently requested data and needs to be particularly fast.

- **Disk cache memory**: part of the disk used to back up the RAM. It often holds up to 40 Mb and enables swapping between the disk and RAM when the latter does not have enough memory to carry out its task.

- **Central memory**: synonymous with random access memory (RAM).

- **Conventional memory**: first part of the DOS memory from 0 to 640 kb.

- **Main memory**: hard disk.

- **EDO (*Extended Data Output*) memory**: allows the processor to access information more quickly.

- **Extended memory**: under DOS, memory situated beyond 1 Mb.

- **Flash memory**: memory used in laptops because of its low power consumption.

- **Graphics memory**: 12-ns high-speed memory used on graphics cards.

- **Upper memory:** under DOS, memory between 640 and 1,024 kb.

- **Read-only memory (ROM)**: fixed, non-volatile memory. It stores programs, particularly those for booting up the computer.

- **Buffer memory**: intermediate memory making it possible to increase the speed of a peripheral or, more rarely, of a program.

- **Random access memory (RAM)**: volatile memory into which you write.

- **Video memory (VRAM)**: memory composed of additional memory chips, sometimes integrated directly on the screen card, which supervises the computer's display. This amount of memory determines the display speed, resolution and number of colours of the screen.

THE CENTRAL MEMORY, OR RANDOM ACCESS MEMORY (RAM)

Let us now clarify a few ideas.

The central memory, also called random access memory (direct access memory) is a volatile memory. It is the memory you use for writing and reading. The information it contains disappears when the central unit is switched off.

It can be used directly by the microprocessor. This memory is measured in thousands of characters.

The unit of memory measurement is the byte, also called a character.

> 1 kb = 1,024 characters (bytes)
>
> 1 Mb = 1,024 × 1,024 characters (bytes)
>
> 1 Gb = 1,024 × 1,024 × 1,024 characters (bytes)

- For running Windows 3.1, your PC requires a minimum of 2 Mb of RAM.

- For running Windows 95, your PC requires a minimum of 16 Mb of RAM.

- For running Windows 98, your PC requires a minimum of 24 Mb of RAM.

- The RAM capacity of a standard PC is 32 to 64 Mb of RAM.

Figure 5.1: SIMM EDO RAM linear arrays

Figure 5.2: 10-ns DIMM SDRAM RAM linear arrays

The RAM linear arrays are plugged into memory expansion slots.

When you go to a shop to buy more basic memory for your PC, you will probably be asked if you want additional linear arrays of 4, 8, 16 or perhaps even 32 Mb. You will be asked if you want a particular speed to match that of your currently installed memory. This is usually too complicated for most users, even those with some experience of computers.

For some time, the trend has been towards simplification, especially when you are equipped with standard hardware. A reputable dealer should be able to advise you on your purchase.

The minimum amount of memory

How much memory is needed to run the CD-ROM or software that you buy?

As a rule, the minimum amount of memory is shown on the package of the software or CD-ROM. The memory used is kept as low as possible so that owners of older PCs operating under Windows 3.1 are able to buy the products. The only exception to this rule are 3D games, which have a high memory requirement.

Drawn in a box, this information is found under the heading 'System requirements' somewhere on the packaging box. For example, a recent documentary-type software would require:

* A 486 PC or higher

* Windows 3.1 in extended mode or Windows 95 or 98

- 8 Mb of RAM
- 10 Mb of disk space
- A mouse
- A colour or black and white printer
- A CD-ROM drive

These are minimum figures. Remember that, since most users do not have the latest computer, CD-ROM authors will adapt their product to the market by taking older models into account.

Division of the RAM

The random access memory, or RAM, is divided into three main categories:

- Conventional memory: memory consisting of the first 640 kb.
- Upper memory: memory situated between the conventional memory and the first megabyte (from 640 to 1,024 kb).
- Extended or high memory: memory situated beyond the first megabyte (above 1,024 Mb).

There is another category which merits special attention. Memory between 64 and 128 Mb creates problems for certain top-of-the-range configurations. There is a bug which, under certain conditions, drastically reduces computer performance. Fortunately it only affects Windows 95 machines and has been eradicated in Windows 98.

Precautions

If you have been working for any length of time, the first precaution to be taken is to save your work on hard disk or diskette. You are then saving it on what is called the 'main memory'.

If you write your text without saving it, everything which was stored in the RAM, which is a volatile memory, disappears when you switch off the PC.

What memory does my PC have?

If you are working under Windows 98 or 95, to find out how much memory your PC has you should:

1. Click on the Start command button.

2. Select Settings.

3. Choose Control Panel.

4. Double-click on the System icon.

5. Click on the Performance tab of the System Properties dialog box. This tab gives you information concerning the amount of memory available on your computer and shows you, for example, the following items:

- **Memory**: 24 Mb of RAM

- **Virtual memory**: 32 bits

- **System resources**: 78% free. If this percentage of available memory is not sufficiently high, the computer could well run too slowly or even stop.

Another way of finding out the amount of memory available on your computer is to look at the screen at start-up. When the PC checks the state of the memory, it displays the number of bytes present.

Virtual memory is hard disk space used as additional RAM memory.

READ-ONLY MEMORY (ROM)

ROM or *Read-Only Memory* (memory for reading only) is memory which is fixed and non-volatile, even when the computer is switched off. The ROM contains programs which provide:

- Start-up

- Internal tests

- Operating system search (Boot or Bootstrap)

The information in ROM can be neither erased nor modified.

The amount of ROM is determined by the manufacturer. You cannot add any. However, you should be able to change it for a more recent version.

 The computer permanently contains a program known as a Bootstrap, which is an initial loading program. This program is placed in ROM by the manufacturer and is started automatically when the computer is powered up. This is what loads the operating system.

CACHE MEMORY

Electronic engineers have invented various tricks for optimising the operation of today's PCs.

These computers are as powerful as the Cray, a giant computer which came out in 1976 and was at the time considered incredibly powerful.

Intermediate storage units, called *cache memory*, have been inserted between the processor and the RAM to serve as buffer memory. They could be compared to small temporary warehouses intended to increase the operational flexibility of the main factory.

This cache memory exists at several levels. The first is situated inside the processor itself, which in this way optimises its internal work transparently. Next comes an external cache in the proximity of the processor, the size of which varies between 64 and 512 kb. This memory is much faster than the normal RAM of the central unit. It is therefore much more expensive. If the RAM has a response speed of 60 ns, that is 60 thousand millionths of a second or a possible 16.7 million responses each second, then the cache memory is five times faster. This is at least the case with first-generation Pentiums. On Pentium IIs, the memory has been improved to such an extent that they have a speed of 10 ns or even less.

Graphics cards have just as powerful a memory, in order to take the load off the central processing unit, which often has a good many images to deal with. A good graphics card will easily support 4 Mb but can even go up to 12 Mb.

If there is insufficient memory at one or other of these levels, the most powerful computer will not live up to its promise.

THE MOTHERBOARD

Inside the central unit is a motherboard on which the microprocessor (see Hour 1), the memory, the expansion slots and the connectors are arranged. The slots make it possible to connect various other cards, such as video cards, controller cards, sound cards and memory cards for adding more random access memory.

Generally the motherboard contains four small slots making it possible to plug in random access memory linear arrays. Because the number of these slots is limited, it is better to choose linear arrays of large capacity, for example, 16 Mb, 32 Mb or even 64 Mb, from the start.

Certain computers allow you to combine two linear arrays with different capacities. Where the speed which distinguishes them is different, the system, if it is sufficiently advanced, aligns itself to the lowest speed so as to avoid synchronisation problems.

Layout of the motherboard

- **Microprocessor or CPU (*Central Processing Unit*)**: the computer's brain (see Hour 1).

- **Arithmetic co-processor**: installed on old machines up to the 386, this is an electronic circuit which speeds up the processing of mathematical operations (see Hour 1). Since the 486 generation, these functions have been integrated into the microprocessor.

- **Expansion slots**: connectors, also called sockets, into which you can plug expansion cards, for example modem cards, fax cards, sound cards, SCSI cards, etc.

- **Random access memory slots**: connectors in which the random access memory or RAM linear arrays are fixed.

- **Keyboard connector**: socket allowing the keyboard cable to be plugged in.

Figure 5.3: The motherboard with microprocessor, memory and expansion slots

- **Connectors for the serial or parallel ports**: slots into which ribbon cables carrying the information can be plugged.

- **Disk connectors**: these allow connection of the hard disk(s).

Figure 5.4: A motherboard

Expandability

Expandability is a computer's capacity for receiving additional peripherals and memory.

The expandability of your PC depends on three parameters:

1. The memory expansion possible

2. The free expansion slots present on the motherboard

3. The external expansion ports

Figure 5.5: Expandability on the motherboard

Figure 5.6: The expansion slots on the motherboard

Figure 5.7: Keyboard and mouse ports

Hour 6

The hard disk

THE CONTENTS FOR THIS HOUR

- The structure of a hard disk
- The characteristics of a hard disk
- A, B, C, D, E
- Formatting a hard disk
- The different types of hard disk
- The hard disk controller cards
- ScanDisk
- Installing a second hard disk
- Housekeeping on your hard disk
- A tough customer

Hard disks make it possible to store and backup large amounts of data, millions (Mb), perhaps even thousands of millions (Gb) of bytes. They are composed of a fixed magnetised disk and a mechanism enabling them to be read.

The current standards are as follows:

- 2.1 Gb
- 3.2 Gb
- 4.3 Gb
- 6.4 or 6.5 Gb
- 8.0 Gb
- 9.0 Gb

The development of multimedia has made it necessary to manufacture disks capable of storing large volumes. Whether it is games, music, video clips or video editing, new formats create new requirements, which is why start-of-the-range disks rarely hold less than 2.1 Gb.

THE STRUCTURE OF A HARD DISK

The structure of the hard disk is the same as that of a diskette: except in the case of large volumes, different disks are stacked one on top of another and enclosed in a case. A disk is characterised by its number of platters (also known as cylinders).

Each disk is covered with a thin magnetisable film (brown oxide or pure metal vapour).

The plates turn around an axis, generally at a speed of 3,600 revolutions per minute.

A read/write head reads data from or writes data to the magnetised surface.

The head sends out a magnetic beam. It never touches the surface and is placed at a distance of 0.0005 mm.

The read heads are assembled on a kind of comb.

The hard disk assembly is supervised by the controller card.

Figure 6.1: A hard disk

Figure 6.2: The plates of the hard disk

The FAT (File Access Table) guides the read heads to the location where the data are arranged in the form of blocks or in segments.

THE CHARACTERISTICS OF A HARD DISK

- **Capacity**: the memory space capacity, also called storage space, is the volume of data which can be recorded on the hard disk. This is the most important item to be taken into consideration when one purchases a hard disk. Opt for a capacity two or three times greater than you actually expect to use.

  The unit of measurement is the Gbyte or Gb, that is a capacity of one thousand million bytes.

- **Access time**: the time necessary for the read head to find the exact spot where the data are situated. It is of the order of a few milliseconds.

A disk-caching program enables you to speed up the mean access time of a hard disk. Windows 98 and 95 have integrated disk-caching programs.

- **Latency time**: the time during which the computer waits before reading the data. It is a few milliseconds.

- **Data transfer speed**: the number of data items which can be transmitted from the hard disk to the memory during one unit of time. The unit of measurement is Mbits/s (millions of bits per second). The data transfer speed is on average 10 Mbits/s (just over 1.2 Mb per second).

- **Interlacing**: the number of rotations of the hard disk for reading all the sectors on a track.

A, B, C, D, E

The floppy disk drives and the hard disks are represented in the File Manager by alphabetic letters followed by a colon.

- **A**: symbolises the first floppy disk drive.

- **B**: symbolises the second floppy disk drive. If you haven't got one, the letter B will remain unused.

- **C**: represents the first hard disk.

- **D**: represents the second hard disk if present. Each new hard disk has an additional letter assigned to it.

- **E**: generally represents the CD-ROM drive.

And so on.

Note: you are strongly recommended to insert your CD-ROM last. Failure to heed this advice may prevent your computer from functioning properly when you install a new hard disk.

Depending on your requirements, it easy to reach the letter G or even H. All you would need, for example, would be three hard disks, one of which was partitioned (C:, D:, E: and F:), an external Iomega Zip drive (G:) and a CD drive (H:).

FORMATTING A HARD DISK

Formatting segments the hard disk into tracks and into tapered sectors. The track corresponds to a circle, the sector to a portion of track. The size of the sector depends on the context. It is not less than 256 bytes but may be much larger.

The address of the file corresponds to a track reference and a sector reference. The location is recorded in a file allocation table (the FAT) on the disk.

The hard disk is preformatted when you purchase your computer.

If you are a novice, it is preferable that you have your hard disk formatted by an expert.

Figure 6.3: The tracks and sectors of the hard disk

THE DIFFERENT TYPES OF HARD DISK

- **External hard disk**: a system which is little used. The hard disk is physically located on the outside of the case of the computer. It is especially used as a backup system (streamer or Bernoulli). In the early days, some disks were external because of their size. A single 20 Mb disk could weigh up to 40 kilogrammes. Today there are fewer reasons to justify external disks, unless these have to be shared between several machines. In 1983, a Bull hard disk containing 20 Mb (10 Mb of which were exchangeable) cost £6,300. Today, the price has dropped ten thousand fold, with £600 getting you 3 disks each with 6.5 Gb of memory, that is one thousand times more space for ten times less money!

- **Internal hard disk**: this is installed inside the computer.

- **Hard disk on a card**: this type of hard disk appeared in 1985. A single electronic card includes the 3½″ format hard disk and its controller. The whole thing connects into one or two free slots on the computer.

The Bernoulli involves a technique which consists of making a flexible system rigid by turning it at very high speed. It has a very large storage capacity. Iomega Corporation was the pioneer of this technology and models were available on the microcomputer market from the 1980s. Daniel

Bernoulli (1700 – 1782) was a Swiss physicist known for a theorem published in 1738 in which he maintained that at any point in a pipe where a fluid under pressure is flowing, the equivalent of the law of conservation of energy is observed.

The streamer is a tape drive using magnetic tapes for the storage of large amounts of data.

The well-known makes

- IBM
- Conner
- Maxtor
- Western Digital
- Quantum
- Seagate

THE HARD DISK CONTROLLER CARDS

A controller card is devoted to controlling and driving a peripheral. It performs information switching functions with conversion and error management.

The controller cards indicate how the information is stored on the hard disk, that is in what order and over what length the digital data have to be converted on the hard disk into magnetic pulses. This operation is known as *encoding*, the reverse operation *decoding*.

ScanDisk

ScanDisk is a software program integrated into Windows 95 which is responsible for checking the state of the hard disk. It analyses the state of the disks you select. It can carry out a standard or thorough analysis depending on your requirements.

- **Standard analysis**: ScanDisk checks files and folders.

- **Thorough analysis**: ScanDisk performs a standard test and checks the disk surface.

- **Advanced options**. These make it possible, for example, to convert fragments of lost files.

Figure 6.4: The ScanDisk tool dialog box

You can also ask it to repair errors. ScanDisk can work as a background task, that is it can run while you are working on another program. This dual task management is, however, to be avoided.

At the end of the analysis, ScanDisk draws up for you a highly accurate report of the errors it detected and the state of the disk it analysed.

Figure 6.5: The advanced ScanDisk options

Accessing ScanDisk

To access ScanDisk, carry out the following operations:

1. Click on Start.

2. Open the Programs option.

3. Select Accessories.

4. Click on System Tools.

5. Select ScanDisk.

Figure 6.6: The ScanDisk report

ScanDisk is useful for repairing errors that occur when you switch off your computer without following the normal Shut Down procedure.

INSTALLING A SECOND HARD DISK

Today's ever more numerous multimedia applications require a significant amount of space on the computer. The installation of one or more additional 2 to 6 Gb hard disks therefore quickly proves essential.

How should you go about it?

1. Switch off and unplug your computer.

2. Remove the cover.

3. Fix the disk under the first hard disk using the screws provided for that purpose.

4. Insert the free flat connector of the cable from the first hard disk into the second hard disk, known as the 'slave'.

5. Connect a free power supply connector into the plug, consisting of four large pins.

6. Put back the cover.

7. Plug in the computer again.

As a rule the PC must recognise the characteristics of your new hard disk.

This operation seems easy to carry out; however, it is better to entrust it to an expert if you are a complete novice!

HOUSEKEEPING ON YOUR HARD DISK

Your housekeeping will be done all the more quickly and correctly if your hard disk is well organised, with explicit directory names, clear and logical filing, and a well-defined tree structure.

1. Your hard disk contains backup copies which you no longer need as '.bak' extensions. Do not hesitate to delete them.

2. Your hard disk contains originals which are no longer of great use to you but which you are keeping as a precaution. The most simple thing to do is to make a copy of them on diskette and archive them, then to destroy the files which are on your hard disk so that you avoid useless clutter as the months go by!

3. Programs produce temporary files. They use the hard disk therefore as a working memory, which is not its true function here since that is the purpose of RAM. The extension of these files is '.tmp'. Most of the time, your computer will do the housekeeping on its own and will delete these files itself once the program is exited, but this is not always the case, particularly if you close down your computer in an illegal manner by directly switching off the computer without first closing the program.

A few solutions for getting rid of these files are as follows.

- Check the status of the files. You will see immediately whether or not they are '.tmp' files.

- If necessary initiate a Find function.

- Click on Explorer.

- Once in the File Manager, open the Tools menu.

- Select the Find option.

- Double-click on Files or Folders.

- Initiate a search not only on the C drive but in all other drives. To do this, use the Find field in the Find All dialog box.

- Enter "*.tmp" in the Named field of the Find All dialog box.

Figure 6.7: Your hard disk is your PC's filing cabinet

A TOUGH CUSTOMER

Of all the components of your installation, the hard disk is certainly the one which has the longest life-expectancy. It contains all the important data, applications, files and the operating system. It runs at 3,600 revolutions per minute, several hours a day, every day. It will without doubt outlive your computer.

Nevertheless, if it were to be damaged, by an electrical storm for example, this would be potentially catastrophic for you, given that the hard disk contains all your files, representing a significant amount of work. Never forget to make copies on diskette of the documents which seem the most important to you. Top-of-the-range Zip or Jaz backup disks can hold 100 Mb, 200 Mb or even 1 Gb.

If the FAT (*File Allocation Table*) is destroyed by the action of a virus, for example, complete chaos appears on your hard disk: there is no longer any consistency and nothing is readable any more. An error message then appears on the screen 'Sector not found'. In that case, there is only one thing to do: switch off the computer and restart with the emergency toolkit. Effective repair softwares include ScanDisk or Disk Doctor. Another solution is the backup FAT. On a hard disk, you find two FATs as a rule. Make a copy of the good FAT in order to repair the damaged FAT.

THE FUTURE

Hard disks have become more compact, less expensive and benefit from improved transfer rates thanks to interfaces which have become increasingly more powerful. For example, Ultra DMA, Ultra DMA/66, Wide SCSI or Ultra2 SCSI (80 Mb/s flow) hard disks use technologies which are innovative today but will be standard tomorrow.

Hour 7

The operating system

THE CONTENTS FOR THIS HOUR

- What is an operating system?
- MS-DOS
- Windows 3.1
- Windows 95
- Windows 98
- Unix and Linux

WHAT IS AN OPERATING SYSTEM?

The operating system is responsible for linking the applications and the hardware.

It is a set of programs responsible for ensuring the correct vital operation of the computer and for managing the peripherals.

Here are a few of the tasks for which the operating system is responsible:

- Formatting diskettes
- Copying files
- Renaming files
- Destroying files
- Displaying a list of programs
- Displaying a list of folders
- Checking the available memory
- Launching and running programs
- Moving from one application to another
- Managing the overall coherence of the system

MS-DOS

In the beginning, MS-DOS was the most widespread operating system for IBM PC-compatible microcomputers in the world. Created by the American publisher Microsoft, it was supplanted first by Windows 3.1, then by Windows 95, both originating from the same workshop as their predecessor.

Since the success of MS-DOS lasted more than a decade, it merits a few lines of description, especially since it lies at the heart of Windows 98 and 95. Even today you need to use DOS to run these programs. Many high-quality games and applications run only on DOS.

You need to have at least a certain knowledge of DOS, if only because it is required for running a good number of tasks. For example, if you wanted to print the contents of a directory or recover it in a text file, you would have to give the instruction in DOS. To launch a DOS session, choose Programs from the Start menu, and, once in DOS, type in the relevant instruction. For example:

    DIR C:\ /S> C:\TEMP\REP01.TXT

This instruction allows you to recover the C drive descriptor, sorted by the option /S, in a text file called REP01 located in the C:\TEMP directory.

Similarly, if Windows breaks down, the boot disk enables action to be taken in DOS mode. It is therefore a good idea to at least have a basic knowledge of how DOS works or to have someone around you who does.

Single-user and single-task

MS-DOS is a single-user and single-task system, which means that it can be used only by a single user and for a single task at any one time. If several users wish to work together, they must be connected in a network.

Start-up

MS-DOS is installed on the hard disk (mass memory). On power-up, MS-DOS is automatically loaded into the memory and invites you to enter a command as soon as the following prompt appears on the screen: C > or C:\>

The main files

The three main files which make up MS-DOS are:

- **MSDOS.SYS**: a hidden file, that is one not listed and not visible by means of the usual commands.

- **IO.SYS**: a hidden file, that is one not listed and not visible by means of the usual commands.

- **COMMAND.COM**: comprises the internal commands loaded automatically when MS-DOS is started. These commands are permanently present in the random access memory, the RAM, and can therefore be used at any time.

The main commands

- **DIR**: directory is a request to display the structure of the disk. It makes it possible to find out how the data are organised on the disk or diskette.

- **FORMAT**: formatting is the command for preparing a diskette which is going to be divided into tracks and into sectors of fixed size so as to receive information.

- **COPY**: the command which makes it possible to copy from one location to another.

- **DEL**: delete is the file destruction command.

- **MD**: make directory creates a directory or subdirectory to be made active.

- **CD**: change directory allows a new directory or subdirectory to be made active.

- **RD**: remove directory makes it possible to remove a directory or subdirectory.

- **CHKDSK**: check disk makes it possible to check the state of the disk.

Operating System may be abbreviated to OS.

How should you access the DOS commands?

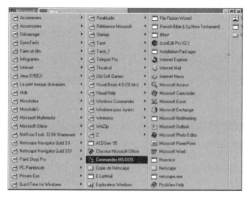

Figure 7.1: The MS-DOS Commands option gives access to a DOS session

1. Click on the Start command in the Taskbar.

2. Select the Programs option

3. Click on MS-DOS Commands.

4. Enter your command at the prompt.

WINDOWS 3.1

Created in 1988, Windows 3.1 constituted an advanced graphical interface which enhanced DOS.

At the time, Windows was not yet an operating system in itself. It would only become so with the 95, 98 and NT versions.

For the first time on PC, the 3.1 version of Windows brought to the screen a quality of presentation to rival that of its competitor, Apple.

It offered multi-windowing, intensive use of the mouse, the simultaneous presence of several programs (only one of which could be active at any one time) and many other features which were to appear with the emergence of different versions, such as Windows 3.1 and Windows 3.11 for Workgroups (Intranet).

At the same time, the leading Microsoft programs, principally Word and Excel, were to benefit from the same development since from now on documents could be shared.

After a slow start due mainly to the relatively low power of the first machines, Windows was quickly to establish itself. Whereas under DOS use of the mouse was limited, it was to become essential under Windows. Drag and Move, Drag and Drop, Copy and Paste, and Cut and Paste were to become major features.

The principles brought into play were to sow the seed of the OLE technology, which, under Windows 95, has been progressively adapted to the Internet under the name ActiveX.

All the new features provided by Windows from Version 3 onwards have been characterised by a flexibility and fluidity which lead to an intuitive user interface. At the same time, certain simple manoeuvres, such as mouse movements, have been enhanced and made more sophisticated. For example, Microsoft has introduced the Intellisense technology, making the mouse intelligent.

Use of the right mouse button has grown, allowing access to advanced functions such as the activation of context-sensitive menus which hang near the spot which is clicked on. In this way, using a number of optimised movements, you can access menus, commands and options without going through the menu bar situated at the top of the screen. Better still, the mouse has become programmable and even context-programmable, which means that the same action will be different depending on the program in use. Overall, you can think of your PC as being as simple to use as the Macintosh but costing less and offering more power. Although in the beginning it was difficult to run Version 3.0 because of numerous and sometimes disheartening bugs, Version 3.1 remedied these drawbacks and won over the public.

WINDOWS 98, 95 AND NT

Windows 95, Windows 98 and Windows NT, the new generation, use the same principles but with different aims and power. Windows 95 is directed at the PC whereas NT aims to become the operating system of future machines and platforms.

Although Version 3 of Windows could multi-task, it could only do so to a limited extent. The applications were active only in turn, even though certain background printing jobs could run at the same time, showing what was to come. Each application present could be accessed simultaneously by striking the sequence of keys ALT + TAB. However, if you exited an Excel application during a long job recalculating a folder and switched to Word or File Manager, the previously exited application ceased to function even if it was still present. Windows 95 really does multi-task. The term is known as pre-emptive multi-tasking, which means that the operating system devotes a fixed and constant time to each application. A master system manages time sharing, making sure that no program forgets to hand back control, which was often the case in the previous version.

At the same time, Windows 95 and 98 provide access to the Internet: first with the Windows Plus accessory software, then with improved versions which came out in the second half of 1996.

New facilities are characterised by progressive adaptation to the principles of the Internet, opening up the system to more extensive sharing of data with the outside world. The set of connection tools included in the new versions facilitate connection and make

extensive use of electronic mail and standardised data exchange in all its forms, to the point that the graphical interface of Windows 98 looks just like that of the Internet, sometimes making it difficult for users looking at their screen to establish the difference between what belongs to their hard disk and what belongs to the outside world.

The numerous improvements which are appearing require greater and greater power. The new operating systems work much better on Pentium 120s and higher equipped with 32 Mb of RAM and a 2- to 4-Gb hard disk. As for the systems being comfortable to use, this is improving substantially. The peripherals are benefiting from the same progress. The screens, in particular, deliver the advertised performance only if they are accompanied by powerful graphics cards with 2 to 4 Mb of 12-nanosecond high-speed graphics memory. Otherwise, displaying becomes excessively slow, and it is irritating to navigate between two Internet sessions in order to display graphics. It could be said that Windows and its hardware are evolving as a function of one other, one pulling the other upwards, and vice versa, creating new markets each time.

NT differs from Windows 95 or 98 in the fact that it works on more powerful platforms intended to intercommunicate by means of networks and offer their power to other machines in a client/ server relationship. For the moment, the products working under NT do not run under Windows 95 or 98, and vice versa. In the future, the versions look likely to merge, which was planned for right from the start. Microsoft has, in a way, avoided repeating the error which, due to lack of power, had slowed the spread of Windows 3.1. However, note that Windows NT is no longer backwards-compatible with DOS. The fact that it does not have to support DOS makes it more powerful.

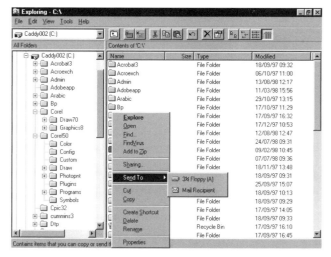

Figure 7.2: The user-friendly Windows 95 interface

THE BENEFITS OF WINDOWS 98

Windows 98 is a not a new concept but rather a collection of small improvements providing a range of services and paving the way for Windows NT, which is destined to rule in the near future.

The new Windows 98 interface, which is oriented towards the use of 'pages', makes it easier to access files and the Control Panel and to customise the Start menu. Once everything is installed, there is the advantage that upgrades are available from the Internet, which gives users more autonomy. If you get a computer bug or a version is improved, all you need to do is download the changes and install them.

Another major advance is the FAT 32, which has increased the available disk space by replacing the basic 32 kb blocks with smaller 4 kb ones. This reduces the space which was previously lost and thus optimises the read-write speed. It has been confirmed that, on a 2 Gb disk containing 16,000 files, including a large number of small images, a FAT 32 provided between 20 to 25% more memory, which is more than 400 Mb. Using the FAT 32 does not result in a loss of data. The system carries out the conversion transparently, provided that the disks have enough free space (approximately one quarter of the surface of the disk) for the work to be carried out.

Eight screens at the same time

A major innovation, which brings Windows 98 closer to UNIX systems, has been the ability to have several screens open at the same time in order to monitor an application. Developers can have one screen for coding, one for developing windows and another for testing programs. Games fanatics can have, for example, an overall screen and a screen showing an enlarged section of their game. It is also possible to have several applications running at once in order to monitor the progress of tasks.

Improved register bases

Register bases can be better handled.

Improved disk drive performance

Disk drives now function faster because the software which drives them has been improved.

New drivers

Windows 98 incorporates several hundred new modem, screen, printer, network card and other drivers.

▰▰▰ Better management of USB peripherals

Under Windows 95, it was neither easy to install nor to manage the USB. This fault has been remedied.

▰▰▰ Better error detection

In the case of what is known as a fatal error, the Doctor Watson program will detect the error in a more user-friendly manner than before by providing the necessary details to understand the error.

▰▰▰ For the experts

To be on the safe side, Windows 98 must be able to be reinstalled using a boot disk which manages the high memory. Note that, if the Windows 98 boot disk does not do so, you must prepare it yourself. Here are the steps and code which must be followed in order to obtain the 445 kb or so that are required under DOS.

1. Use a standard Windows 95 (not Windows 98) boot disk

2. In the Config.sys program, add the following lines using a text editor:

   ```
   device=c:\windows\himem.sys
   device=c:\windows\emm386.exe noems
   dos=high, umb
   ```

3. Replace all the 'device' instructions with 'devicehigh'

4. In the Autoexec.bat program, load the resident programs into the high memory using the Load High (LH) instruction. For example, to load the driver required to use the Windows 98 installation CD-ROM, type in:

   ```
   lh a:\MSCDEX.EXE /D:MTMIDE01 /L:G
   ```

5. Do not forget to resave the Autoexec.bat and Config.sys programs.

6. Install Windows 98 using the install program in the \codefr\ directory of the Windows 98 CD-ROM.

This will stop the system repeatedly refusing to install itself because of insufficient memory. If in doubt, contact a friend with some computer knowledge or a computer supplier.

UNIX AND LINUX

Invented in 1970 in the Bell Laboratories, by Ken Thompson and Kernigan Richtie, Unix and the C Language put a stamp on their era by spreading computer knowledge both in American universities and in companies. The first to be created was the C Language, which was used to write the Unix operating system. This progressively established itself as the language of computing in an age when even the idea of micro-computing could not yet be conceived. Because Unix and C were the dominant languages taught at university, they became the most commonly used by computer engineers.

For this reason, as soon as the power of PCs allowed it, a number of users preferred to install Unix on their PC. At the same time, a strand of thought from the United States, extolling completely free software programs and operating systems, progressively established itself and gave rise to a family of products which were, at the same time, free, high-performing and evolutionary. Among these were GNU and Linux.

The free part of Unix, GNU, represents, as it were, a recursive acronym for GNUs not Unix.

Linux, which is also free, is very similar and has become increasingly more widespread on PCs, with more and more books being written on the subject.

Today, you are recommended to use Windows 98 or Windows 95 in order to take advantage of the numerous multimedia possibilities of the software available. Although many users remain faithful to Windows 3.1 or enjoy using Linux, the future is likely to belong to Windows 98 and NT.

Figure 7.3: Icons contribute towards making an operating system user-friendly

Hour 8

Multimedia

THE CONTENTS FOR THIS HOUR

- The features of multimedia
- The sound card
- The graphics card
- The CD-ROM
- The DVD-ROM
- Many hands make light work
- The scanner
- The digital camera

THE FEATURES OF MULTIMEDIA

Multimedia is the combination of sound, words and pictures to create stunning aesthetic effects, allowing you to explore and develop your creative talent.

Combining the senses

In his book *The Doors of Perception*, Aldous Huxley explains the phenomenon of synaesthesia, making one sense correspond to another sense. Today, thanks to multimedia, you can buy CD-ROMs which allow you to do just that. For example, there are ground-breaking CD-ROMs out now in the shops which allow you to listen to a musical piece by Debussy, read a text by Verlaine and admire a watercolour painting by Monet on your computer screen all at the same time.

Creativity and play

A computer equipped with a CD-ROM drive and sound card is a computer which allows you to learn and play. The play dimension of multimedia no longer needs to be proved. Just look at the figures and you'll get an idea: of CD-ROM sales in 1995, games represented 57% of the market, art and culture 22%, education 16% and erotica 5%.

A multimedia computer

To support a multimedia installation, your computer must first have the following minimum characteristics:

- A PC with a 486 or Pentium processor with 256 kb of cache memory

- At least 16 Mb of RAM

- SVGA graphics screen card

- 16-bit sound card

- External speakers
- 500-Mb hard disk

This means that you don't necessarily need the latest model of computer to support multimedia.

Figure 8.1: Your multimedia PC

THE SOUND CARD

The sound card plugs into an expansion slot on the motherboard. This is what converts analogue data (sound) into digital data (the sound file). All sound cards have connectors for the microphone inputs, and outputs to the enclosures. The SoundBlaster is an established make.

You also use the sound card for connecting your computer to speakers, microphones and musical instruments compatible with the MIDI standard.

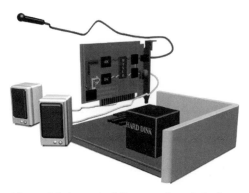

Figure 8.2: Layout of the sound cards in the central unit

Sound files

The WAV format is the standard for Windows sound files on PCs. However, much better is the MP3 format, which is compressed ten times without a loss in quality. 1 Mb of MP3 corresponds to approximately one minute of sound. This means you can get approximately twelve hours of music, including the spoken word, on one single CD. The MP3 is in the course of being replaced by the even more powerful MP4.

There are other standards on the market, particularly the ASJ, AU or Real Audio (.ra) formats, which allow access to some radio stations via the Internet. However, there is little chance that these will displace MP3 as the standard format.

Musical files

The MIDI (*Musical Instrument Digital Interface*) standard is a system for communicating between the computer and musical instruments. Each action of the musician is coded and sent to the computer via the case. This standard is almost universal for music on its own, but does not reproduce the human voice, as it is actually the notes that are coded.

More and more PCs have a MIDI connector, a consequence of the increasing success of multimedia.

THE GRAPHICS CARD

The graphics card is a card which makes it possible to work creatively (receiving/sending) and which manages your screen. This card translates the signals handled by the monitor into a format which the monitor can display.

In general, this screen card is integrated into the motherboard. Sometimes, it is an expansion card which is plugged into one of the expansion slots.

The image processing speed determines the number of colours which can be displayed.

The memory capacity of screen cards is on average 1 Mb or more, supporting up to 16.7 million colours with a resolution of 640×480 pixels.

The SVGA card

SVGA cards represent the current standard. They add the 800×600 and 1024×768 graphics modes to the VGA card capabilities. With a suitable card driver, you can display up to 1600×1200.

There are various graphics cards which specialise in either 2D or 3D. There is no point in purchasing a 3D card such as a 3DFX II if you do not use your computer to play games or create computer-generated images.

A good card has a graphics memory of between 4 and 12 Mb. This comfortably allows you to properly run graphics programs, which always require a large amount of memory.

THE CD-ROM

CD-ROM means *Compact Disc Read Only Memory*. ROM, or *Read Only Memory*, cannot be erased or rewritten, and allows reading only. The CD-ROM stores any type of digitised information, that is information translated into binary, 0s and 1s, the language which the computer understands.

Figure 8.3: Multimedia equipment: the CD-ROM with its accessories and sound card

Storage

The CD-ROM has a storage capacity of 650 Mb of data, which corresponds to around one hundred books on a single disk.

Installation

Once you have slid your CD-ROM into the CD-ROM drive, how do you install it?

- **The Device Manager**: the components of the computer, whether CD-ROM drives or graphics cards, for example, are managed by a software program called the *Device Manager*. This must be configured, that is programed, to fetch the data from the peripherals.

- **Install.exe**: there are two types of CD-ROM: those which run as soon as they are put into the drive and those which require information to be first installed on the computer.

- **The importance of Quicktime**: in order to display video sequences, the majority of CD-ROMs use the Quicktime software program.

Your version of Quicktime may conflict with the version loaded by the CD-ROM. For this reason, install the most recent version only.

- **Copy as little as possible**: the fewer CD-ROMs you install, the less you will clutter up your hard disk. Complete installation, which copies the application itself and other files as well, may occupy several Megabytes.

- **Uninstall**: the best way of deleting everything after use is to run the Uninstaller program. You can also select Add/Remove Programs in the Windows 95 Control Panel.

CD-ROMs wear out in the course of being used and should be cleaned from time to time. Grease spots or finger marks prevent the disk from being read correctly. CD-ROMs are covered with a very thin plastic film. To clean your CD-ROM wipe it with a clean lint-free cloth in a straight line from centre to edge.

CD-ROM manufacture

CD-ROMs are manufactured as follows:

- **Digitisation**: all the elements which make up the data on the CD-ROM (sound, video, image, text) are translated into digital data.

- **Creation of the glass master**: the digitised data are sent for laser recording. The beam engraves the glass disc (glass master) with a pattern of hollows and bumps corresponding to the 0 and 1 binary data.

- **The nickel original**: from the glass disc, a nickel original called the 'father' is produced. This will be used as a mould.

- **Pressing**: plastic is injected into the mould, pressed and then cooled. The operation lasts four seconds. The digital data are engraved on the plastic disc.

- **Metallisation**: the plastic disc is covered with a thin layer of metal (aluminium) to allow it to be read with a laser beam.

- **Varnishing**: the aluminium layer is covered with a film of varnish.

- **Silk-screen printing**: this makes it possible to illustrate the CD-ROM with a colour image, for example.

Figure 8.4: The CD-ROM

The CD-ROM drive

CD-ROM drives may be installed internally or externally:

- Internally, inside the case, which makes it possible to save space on your desk.

- Externally, with the drive connected to a port located on the central unit.

The CD-ROM drive can be connected in two different ways:

- **IDE ATAPI**: the drive is connected to the IDE controller.

- **SCSI**: the drive forms part of a SCSI chain.

Setting the parameters

To set the multimedia parameters for your installations, carry out the following operations:

1. Click on Start.

2. Select Settings.

3. Select Control Panel.

4. Click on the Multimedia icon.

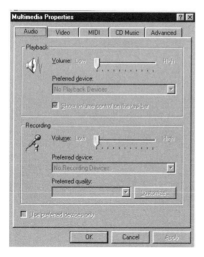

Figure 8.5: The Multimedia Properties dialog box allows you to set the sound, the image and all the multimedia peripherals

The Multimedia Properties dialog box opens on the screen. This contains five tabs:

- Audio

- Video

- MIDI
- CD Music
- Advanced

Speed of rotation

CD-ROM drives differ by their speed of rotation. The oldest models run at a speed of 200 to 535 revolutions/minute, the most recent models between 1680 and 4320 revolutions/minute. During these speeds of rotation, they transfer the digitised data in the form of kilobytes per second (kb/s). The first models had a transmission rate of 150 kb/s, that is they transmitted 150,000 characters per second to the computer. This transmission rate is four to five times greater than that of the hard disk. As it was insufficient for videos, it was necessary to increase the speeds.

- Dual-speed: 2×150, that is 300 kb/s CD-ROM
- Quad-speed: 4×150, that is 600 kb/s CD-ROM
- 8-speed: 8×150, that is 1,200 kb/s CD-ROM
- And so on up to 24 and 32 or 4.8 Mb/s

In 1998, the 24X CD constituted the new standard. However, it should be emphasised that the four-speed CD suffices for the majority of applications.

Reading

Reading the data from the CD-ROM is performed using a laser beam. This scans the surface of the disc in order to interpret the differences in relief corresponding to the binary data: zero = hollow, 1 = filled.

Equipment per family

Multimedia is a sector which is taking off gently.

Figures for the number of homes equipped with microcomputers in 1997 were as follows: United States 37%, Germany 26%, England 23% and France 15%.

The DVD-ROM

The DVD-ROM, or Digital Video Disc, is the size of a CD-ROM: 12 cm in diameter. It stores between 4.7 and 8.5 Gb of data, that is almost 13 times more than the CD-ROM. The DVD-ROM is expected to be on sale shortly. Manufacturers such as Panasonic, Pioneer, Philips, Sony and Toshiba are preparing revolutionary products. The first DVD-ROMs should sell at around £500. Is this to say that the days of the CD-ROM are numbered? Probably. Besides the data storage capacities which are eight times larger than that of the CD-ROM, the DVD-ROM offers unequalled sound and image quality.

Nothing to worry about

DVD-ROM does not herald the end of the CD-ROM. Both use the same format and interface. So what's the difference?

- **The drive**: in order to read a DVD-ROM, you must have a DVD-ROM drive, into which of course you can also insert your CD-ROMs. The DVD-ROM is backwards compatible, so there is no need to throw out your CD-ROM collection.

- **The storage capacity**: the type of data which can be written on this new medium has an effect on its capacity and its mode of operation. This is because the DVD-ROM can store computer data and video films, which occupy much more memory and space.

- The laser for the DVD is 10 times more accurate than that used by the current CD-ROM drives.

Gradual transition

The transition between CD-ROM and DVD-ROM will not be made overnight. Publishers and manufacturers are progressively preparing for this new technological change by devising not only new drives but also computers specially dedicated to the DVD-ROM. The odds are that the conventional Pentium will also quickly become inadequate in the face of this new technology.

MANY HANDS MAKE LIGHT WORK

One single person is not sufficient to produce a CD-ROM. The combined action of different skills means that a close-knit team of at least half a dozen people is necessary.

Figure 8.6: Creation of a CD-ROM: the combined action of different skills

- The author is the creative inspiration behind the product. The author conceives the need for the CD-ROM, designs its features, sketches out a draft and submits it to the publisher. If there is agreement, a contract is signed with the author and production of the CD-ROM will begin. In three months, the CD-ROM may be finished.

- The associate designer helps the author in handling any aspects of content in which the latter is less of an expert. The associate designer will share any profits that are made.

- The programmer works together with the author to sort out aspects relating to programming and creating the CD-ROM interface and is responsible for implementing, point by point, the specification. The programmer is mentioned in the tripartite contract signed with the publishing house.

- The technicians supervise the work of the programmer and check, amongst other things, the effectiveness of the installation program.

- The marketing person, using the catalogue in which the future appearance of the CD-ROM is announced, canvases retail outlets, hypermarkets and specialist shops, presents the product, outlines its area of interest and sometimes performs demonstrations.

- The publisher, given the results of the first quarter's sales, for example, takes the decision to proceed with a second run of 1,000 or 2,000 copies, and to have it translated and marketed in other countries.

Learning to converse

As a rule, everyone who works on the production of a CD-ROM, at whatever level, meet or call one another several times. It is here that an additional area of importance and difficulty lies: it is necessary to learn to converse with people from very different backgrounds, with complementary but sometimes contrasting skills: the design artist with the programmer, the programmer with the technicians, the technicians with the marketing person, the marketing person with the publisher, and the publisher with the author.

SCANNER

The scanner breaks down the work document (photograph, graph, text, etc.) into the form of a series of dots, or pixels, which can be used by the computer. Depending on the amount of light each square contains, the scanner chooses a shade of white or black. The most advanced scanners take grey levels into consideration.

Once the document is digitised and stored on the hard disk, the user can work on it. If it is an image, he or she can rework it using graphics software, making it appear anything he or she wants. Watch out for the caricatures produced from scanned identity photographs!

Digitising the image results in a loss of definition. The greater the increase in number of pixels, the greater the improvement in definition.

Pixel is a contraction of Picture element. The dot is the smallest level of the image. Sixteen grey levels require a pixel of four minipixels a side. Grey is therefore much more difficult to produce than colour.

There are different types of scanner.

- **The flatbed scanner**: this works on the photocopier principle, except that it sends its results to a file instead of printing them on a sheet of paper.

- **The hand-held scanner**: inexpensive, this works very well. It is easily sufficient for scanning small documents, but is unsatisfactory for larger formats, even complete pages.

- **The platen type scanner**: less and less widespread, this is the first-generation scanner. Not very practical, it accepts only detached sheets. One cannot, for example, scan a sheet in a book without cutting it out beforehand, which of course reduces its importance. The platen type scanner, also called a drum scanner, has become an obsolete rarity to be avoided for home use.

It's pointless to spend a fortune on a good scanner for general use;
perfectly satisfactory models may be bought for as little as £300.

Figure 3.13: Text passed under a hand-held scanner

Figure 3.14: The flatbed scanner

THE DIGITAL CAMERA

The digital camera is becoming more popular and a normal consumer model will cost between £150 and £700. The fact that you can buy one for as little as £150 shows how fast the technology is advancing.

If you already have a scanner, what is the advantage of having a digital camera as opposed to a normal model?

- The film is free.

- There is no need to use a scanner to transfer photos.

- You can load your photos directly onto your laptop.

What are the disadvantages?

- It costs more than a conventional camera.

- The resolution is not as good. This is the main drawback.

- You get a limited number of photos. You have to unload the memory card before you can use it again.

A digital camera replaces the film with pixel matrices, each one of which senses light and transmits the results to the memory in the form of a card. The sensors use a technique called CCD (Charged Coupled Device), which converts the light into digital data.

Your photos are stored on flash cards (CompactFlash) or Smartmedia. Some Sony models even have an in-built disk drive. The number of photos you can store depends not only on the definition (the size of the photo in pixels) but also on the compression mode (JPEG) used, which strikes a balance between quality and storage volume.

Start-of-the-range models create photos with a definition of
240 × 320, 480 × 320 or 640 × 480 pixels. However, certain models
have a definition of 493 × 373 or even 765 × 504 pixels, such as
the Kodak DC 25 or DC 50. To obtain high-quality printed photos,
it is better to choose a higher definition (1,024 × 768 pixels or
more). High-quality models, which often have a built-in flash and
zoom, cost less than £500. And for a little more, you can get models
with more than a million pixels plus 8 Mb memory cards and macro-
photography functions. The best-known makes are Canon, Epson,
Casio, Agfa, Kodak and Sony.

Once you have copied your digital or scanned-in photos onto your
computer, you can use one of the many retouching programs
available on the market. By acting on the colour components, these
allow you to improve or 'save' defective documents. For example,
you can improve the appearance of old, poor-quality photographs
and lessen the effect of over- or underexposure and colour shift. It
is for this reason that scanners and digital cameras often come with
these software programs included.

Hour 9

The Internet

THE CONTENTS FOR THIS HOUR

- The computer
- The modem
- The subscription
- The access provider
- The connection

The Internet, which allows you to make contact with people and access information from anywhere in the world, has revolutionised the art of communication, making it simpler, more direct and far more suited to the needs of today. Thanks to its amazing speed, the Internet is able to provide you with almost instant answers to your questions and allows you to converse with people whose geographical distance from you means you would never have met under normal circumstances. What is more, it is so simple that anyone and not just computer programmers can use it. By simply clicking on the mouse, you can obtain information on whatever subject you want, from the latest news to a cooking recipe. More and more people are coming to realise the importance of the Internet as an indispensable information and communication tool. So much so that, in many homes, it is now considered as important to be online as it is to have a phone, television or car.

THE COMPUTER

You can access the Internet with just about any type of computer, whether it is a Mac or a PC. To access the Internet, it is recommended that you have a minimum of:

- A PC with a 75 or Pentium processor.

- A hard disk with a minimum capacity of 500 Mb. While you only need a few tens of Mb for installing the programs needed to gain access to the Internet, you can very quickly download several hundred of them.

- A 16-Mb random access memory which will allow you to open several Internet applications simultaneously (electronic mail, Web, file transfer).

- A SoundBlaster-compatible sound card and speakers if you want to download recordings. The speakers may be integrated or external, with or without bass enclosures. Audio cards are essential for games and CD-ROMs.

- A graphics card.

- A CD-ROM drive: this is essential if you opt for an IAP (Internet Access Provider) which offers you the connection kit on CD-ROM.

- A 15" or 17" screen. These sizes will allow for more comfortable viewing.

A total budget of at least £800.

The modem

The modem ('modulator/demodulator') is one of your PC's peripherals, increasingly being incorporated into the computer. Using it, your PC can communicate with the rest of the network via a telephone line.

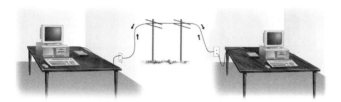

Figure 9.1: The PC communicates with the rest of the network via a telephone line, cable or satellite

Files sent to or received from the Internet pass through your modem. Its quality and price vary according to its data transmission speed, expressed in bits per second (bps). If possible, choose a powerful 56,000 bps modem. The average price of a modem is around £100.

At a speed of 14,400 bps, two pages of text of 1,500 signs will take two seconds to reach their destination. At a speed of 28,800 bps, the transmission time is half as long.

External modem and internal modem

The modem may be external or internal.

- **Internal**: in this case, this comes in the form of a card which can be plugged into a slot.

- **External**: the equivalent of the modem card is incorporated in an external case and connected to the computer by means of a cable fastened to one of the communication ports.

Figure 9.2: An external modem

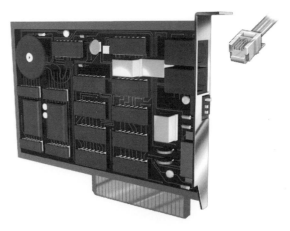

Figure 9.3: An internal modem

▒▒▒▒FAQ (Frequently Asked Question)

Question: Can I install my modem on the same line as my telephone?

Answer: Yes. You can make or receive calls when you are not using the Internet, and therefore your modem, although new techniques will soon allow you to download from the Internet and speak over the phone at the same time. The principle is based on different frequencies.

THE SUBSCRIPTION

There are two types of service offered by access providers:

- **Minimum subscription with connection limited to a few hours**. Every additional hour spent online is relatively expensive.

- **Subscription with unlimited connection**. Obviously you will still receive a telephone bill invoicing you for the number of hours spent online.

Most services offer a mailbox and space for creating your own web pages.

▒▒▒▒ The online services

The simple subscription costs from £5 to £10 per month. For this price, you receive a credit of connection hours to one of the main online servers such as Compuserve or AOL, or to a small (often excellent local server), each one of which will connect you to the network.

These commercial services are large electronic publishing services which offer the conventional Internet services such as electronic mail and newsgroups as well as a fairly extensive range of diverse

information designed and produced by the service itself. You will find among other things:

- Daily newspapers

- Tourist information

- Mail order catalogues

- Games.

One advantage of such commercial services is that they offer you access to their own banks of information, inaccessible to other Web users.

The main drawback of such commercial services is that they invoice everything, from the time of use to the amount of information requested. Each unit of mail is invoiced, as is each unit of connection time.

It is better to start by carefully analysing your needs and taking into account that they might change. You can then choose a suitable solution. However, bear in mind that consumption is rapidly increasing.

THE ACCESS PROVIDER

The IAP (*Internet Access Provider*) gives you the following services for a subscription of £10 to £20 a month:

- No restrictions or charges for the time you spend online

- A connection kit

- A hot line service, that is a telephone support service intended to help you out as soon as you are in difficulty.

Be aware that certain hot line services, or services claiming to be such, can be always busy or impossible to contact.

- At the moment there are around 50 providers in the UK. Some are specific to a particular area of the country and others offer UK-wide coverage.

- All offer e-mail, World Wide Web, FTP, Telnet, Gopher, IRC and newsgroup access. Some offer ISDN and other extras.

- The majority of access providers will offer you local telephone access, which will allow you to contact family and friends the other side of the world for the price of a local call!

If in doubt, ask for advice from members of Internet discussion groups or mailing lists. You will find them to be very well informed and often fiercely opposed to service providers who do not keep their promises. Strangely enough, you will find that some access providers are excellent in some areas (if you live close to an Internet Service Provider) and much less so in others (if you live in area which is not very well served).

THE CONNECTION

Before connecting your modem, you must first configure it.

Configuring your modem

If you have not yet bought your modem, choose an external model if you can, since this leaves a slot free for other extensions (scanners, sound or graphics cards, SCSI cards).

1. Connect your modem to the serial port (COM port) and to a telephone line. If your computer is equipped with an internal modem, you just need to connect it to the telephone socket.

2. Check in the directions for use delivered with your PC that the serial port supports the UART 16550 AF standard provided for high-speed transmission rates.

The following operations are far from straightforward. To carry them out, use the documentation supplied by your access provider, but do not hesitate to enlist the help of a computer friend if necessary.

If you are working with Windows 3.1:

1. Install the modem driver manager using the diskette supplied.

2. Open the Program Manager.

3. Select the Accessories group.

4. Double-click on the Terminal icon.

5. Select the Communications command in the dialog box which is displayed.

6. Define the settings for your modem in the Settings menu: transmission speed, data bits, stop bits, parity and flow control.

If you are working with Windows 95 or 98:

1. Click on the Start icon in the Taskbar.

2. Select the Settings menu.

3. Open the Control Panel submenu.

7. Click on the Add New Hardware icon.

8. The Add New Hardware Wizard opens on the screen.

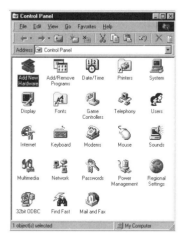

Figure 9.4: The Windows 98 Add New Hardware icon

Figure 9.5: The Add New Hardware Wizard guides you step by step

9. Click on Next. Answer the questions that appear. If your hardware is Plug and Play (which would be logical), Windows 98 will detect it. If not, you will be asked to choose

between automatic detection and selecting from a list. Do not worry about which one you choose; either one will do. Let's say you decide to select from a list.

10. Select the Modem option.

Figure 9.6: Select the Modem option

11. The Install New Modem dialog box informs you that Windows 95 (or 98) is preparing to detect your modem.

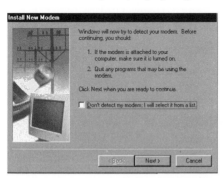

Figure 9.7: If your modem is not recognised as Plug and Play, either choose automatic detection or select one from a list

12. Select the name of your modem manufacturer.

13. Click on Next.

14. Windows copies the data onto your hard disk.

15. You should now indicate which communication port is to be used by the modem. In the majority of cases it is COM2.

    Select COM2.

16. Click on Next.

17. The Location Information dialog box opens on the screen. You must provide information on your current location so that your calls are dialled correctly. You must specify which country you live in and in which telephone area you are situated.

18. Return to the Control Panel.

19. Click on the Modem icon. The Modem Properties dialog box opens on the screen.

20. Click on the Properties tab to configure your hardware.

    - The General tab concerns the settings for the speaker volume and the speed chosen for making the connections.

    - The Connection tab concerns the connection parameters and call parameters.

For the time being, use the default call parameters.

Figure 9.8: The Modem Properties diqalog box

21. Once the Connection tab has been selected, click on the Port Settings command button. This new dialog box enables you to set the size of the buffers.

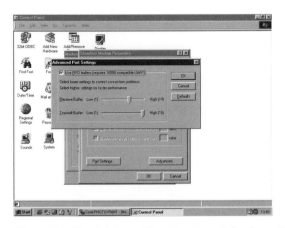

Figure 9.9: The Advanced Port Settings dialog box allows you to adjust the buffer size

▬▬▬ Configuring your connection

Once your connection kit diskettes are installed, the only thing that remains for you to do in order to be connected to the Internet is to enter into your computer the data supplied by your access provider.

What does connecting your computer to the Internet mean? It is quite simply giving it the capability of making contact with other computers on the network. The two keystones of this computer-to-computer dialog are:

- *Internet Protocol* (IP)

- *Transmission Control Protocol* (TCP)

Current terminology speaks of TCP/IP. These two protocols take care of breaking down the information into data packets, transferring them, and then unloading them in the correct order. Here is how to proceed.

With Windows 3.1:

The first operation consists of installing a TCP/IP program suite. With Windows 3.1, the most common is Trumpet Winsock, which you should as a rule find in your connection kit.

1. Start Trumpet Winsock.

2. Select the Setup command from the File menu.

3. Define the transmission protocol in the dialog box which appears on the screen. In the majority of cases, this is Internal PPP.

4. Specify the port used by your modem in the SLIP Port section.

5. Indicate the transmission speed in the Baud Rate section.

6. Specify the ID of your access provider.

7. Specify the gateway used in the Name Server and Default Gateway sections.

8. Click on OK to return to the main menu.

9. Open the Dialler menu.

10. Start the program SETUP.CMD.

11. Enter the telephone number of your access provider in the dialog box which appears on the screen.

12. Confirm by clicking on OK.

13. Enter your user name or login.

14. Confirm by clicking on OK.

15. Enter your password.

16. Close Trumpet Winsock.

17. Restart Trumpet Winsock.

18. Choose the Dialler menu.

19. Select the Login command to activate your connection.

With Windows 95 or 98:

1. Open the Control Panel.

2. Select the Network icon.

3. Click on the Add button of the Network dialog box.

4. Select Protocol in the list then click on Add in the Select Network Component Type dialog box.

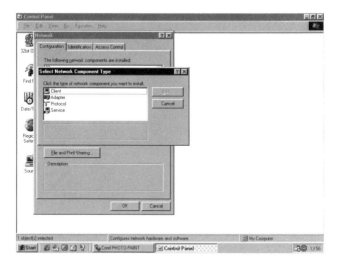

Figure 9.10: Click on the Add option in the Select Network Component Type dialog box. This example allows you to install a modem cable connected to an Ethernet card

5. Choose Microsoft in the Manufacturers section of the dialog box

6. Choose TCP/IP in the Network Protocols scrolling list.

7. Confirm by clicking on OK. You return to the Network dialog box.

8. Select the protocol you have just added.

9. Click on Properties.

10. Select the IP Address tab.

11. Tick the box Obtain an IP Address automatically.

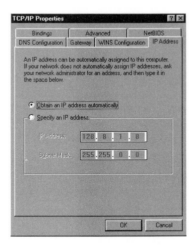

Figure 9.11: Tick the box Obtain an IP Address automatically in the TCP/IP Properties dialog box on the IP Address tab

12. Select the WINS Configuration tab.

13. Select the Disable WINS Resolution option.

14. Select the Gateway tab.

15. Enter the address of your access provider.

16. Click on Add.

17. Select the DNS Configuration tab.

18. In the Domain text field, enter the name of your access provider.

19. In the Host text field, enter your name.

20. In the DNS Server Search Order field, enter the numbers which have been sent to you by your access provider.

21. Confirm by clicking on OK.

22. Close again.

23. Click on the Start command in the Taskbar.

24. Select the Programs menu.

25. Select the Accessories submenu.

26. Click on the Dial-Up Network Access option.

27. Double-click on the New Connection icon.

28. Assign a name to this connection.

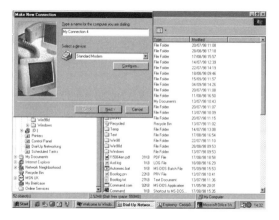

Figure 9.12: The New Connection dialog box enables you to assign a name to your connection

29. Enter the number of the server of your access provider.

30. Click on Finish.

31. Select the Connection icon.

32. Click on Configure.

33. Select the Options tab.

34. Tick the box Bring up terminal window after dialling, then the box Display modem status.

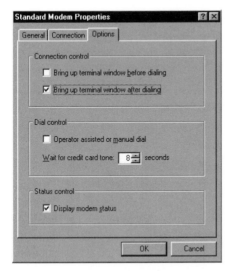

Figure 9.13: Tick the box Bring up terminal window after dialling, then the box Display modem status

35. Open the Connections menu of the Dial-Up Network Access dialog box.

36. Select Dial-Up Access Server.

Figure 9.14: Open the Connections menu of the Dial-Up Network Access dialog box and click on the Dial-Up Access Server option

37. Click on the Server Type command button.

38. Select the TCP/IP protocol.

39. Request the TCP/IP settings.

40. Select the options IP address assigned by server and addresses of the named server assigned by server, Use IP header compression, and finally Use Default Gateway for the Dial-Up Network.

41. Activate your connection by double-clicking on the My Connection icon.

42. A Connection dialog box asks you for your password and user name.

Figure 9.15: The dialog box which allows the connection to be initiated

43. Click on the Connect command button.

44. You will hear the modem dialling while the icon which is situated at the bottom left of the dialog box flickers.

45. You are connected to the Internet.

Hour 10

The work corner

THE CONTENTS FOR THIS HOUR

- Workstation ergonomics
- Sharing a computer
- Visual comfort
- Ambient comfort
- The workstation
- The ten commandments
- Teleworking
- Teleworking occupations
- The status of the teleworker
- The different forms of teleworking

WORKSTATION ERGONOMICS

Ergonomics groups together studies and research on the methodical organisation of work and on the development of equipment adapted to workers' needs. With time, the name ergonomics has also come to cover the quality of life and the comfort of the user. Workstation ergonomics means feeling good when you are working.

▬▬▬ Feeling good about your PC

How can you make PCs – on which the majority of us work for a minimum of eight hours a day – an enjoyable and user-friendly working environment?

SHARING A COMPUTER

The first factor you must take into consideration when choosing an area in which to install your PC is the number of users. Is it a PC which you alone are going to use, or one which you are going to share with other members of the family, your children for example? If this is the case, it is better to organise a place with easy access.

For young users, a sturdy and adjustable chair is essential, as is a solid and resistant keyboard. Do not allow your children to eat or drink while using the keyboard and teach them to leave the computer and accessories such as diskettes and printouts as they found them.

Figure 10.1: The back must be perfectly straight

VISUAL COMFORT

Many people still think that working on a computer damages the eyes. And yet, studies carried out so far do not indicate conclusively that working on a screen harms your eyesight. On the other hand, if you unknowingly suffer from poor eyesight, it is possible that a series of sessions on a computer will reveal it. It is up to you to react and consult an optician. But before worrying you, let us first analyse the various factors involved.

Eye strain

When you use a screen, your eye muscles are forced to work repetitively and intensely. This is why the majority of eye problems caused by the use of computers are related to eye strain. If you feel this type of fatigue coming on, the simplest thing to do is give yourself 15 to 20 minutes' break.

The most common sight problems are the following:

- Redness
- Watering
- Blurred vision

- Double vision

- Headaches

The various causes of your problems may be as follows:

- **Length of time working facing the screen**: two hours continuously facing the screen is inadvisable. It is difficult to draw up valid rules for everybody, so listen to your personal warning signals and take breaks accordingly. Health and safety guidelines recommend taking a break every 20 minutes.

- **Lighting environment**: optimum comfort depends on the contrast and intensity of the light that reflects off the visual fields and surfaces you are using. Indirect lighting (e.g. a halogen lamp pointed towards the ceiling or the wall) is often more pleasant to work in than direct light.

- **Quality of the documents to be input**: the presentation and legibility of documents are not always as good as they could be. Be particular: refuse to type documents if you consider them difficult to read, while, for the benefit of others, remember to produce legible and neat documents yourself.

COMFORTABLE SURROUNDINGS

Here are a few suggestions for obtaining the best possible comfort.

The lighting environment

For optimum comfort, try to observe the following conditions:

- A brightness of the overall visual field which is satisfactory with no reflections on the screen.

- Sufficient contrast between the brightness of the screen background and the brightness of the characters.

- A ratio of brightness between the screen, the document and the peripheral visual field which is not too great to avoid glare.

As a general rule, make sure that the background of your screen is not too dark so that it does not contrast too much with light-coloured work surfaces .

Sources of glare must therefore be excluded entirely:

- The user should not be facing a window.
- The user should not have his back to a window.
- Indirect lighting is essential, together with an anti-glare screen over the monitor.
- Individual lights must be arranged around the work surface.

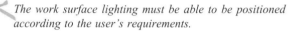

The work surface lighting must be able to be positioned according to the user's requirements.

Lighting

It is advisable to have some sort of movable protection against the sun in the work room:

- Venetian blinds with slats which can be angled
- Mesh fabric blinds
- Net curtains

As regards artificial lighting, there are three types:

- Direct: 90% of radiation downwards
- Semi-direct: 50% of radiation downwards
- Indirect: 90% of radiation upwards

As regards the colours and coverings of your work room, do not use:

- Vivid colours
- Shiny surfaces
- Accentuated geometric shapes

The sound environment

The presence of sources of sound that differ from those generated by the workstation itself can be a disturbing factor for the user.

The consequences of these annoying factors immediately make themselves felt on the person and therefore on the quality of his or her work:

- Headaches

- Tension

- Loss of concentration

- Decrease in the ability to think

- Decrease in productivity

Decibels

The decibel tolerance thresholds are as follows:

- 30 to 40 decibels: quiet

- 50 to 60 decibels: noisy

- 60 to 70 decibels: difficulty hearing over the phone

- 80 decibels and over: very noisy

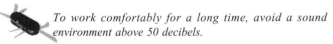

To work comfortably for a long time, avoid a sound environment above 50 decibels.

The noisiest things in a work room are:

- The telephone

- The printer

- The fax machine

There are different ways of reducing the sound intensity of a room and the noisiest work tools:

- Using a sound-proofing device
- Decreasing the telephone ringing volume
- Sound-absorbent telephone booth panels
- Sound-absorbent ceilings
- Insulating walls

The following figures should give you an order of magnitude:

- Desert: 10 decibels
- Recording studio: 20 to 30 decibels
- Quiet house: 30 decibels
- Busy street: 60 decibels
- Inside a sports car: 70 decibels
- Rotary presses: 80 decibels
- The Underground or Niagara Falls: 90 decibels
- Thunder: 100 decibels
- Limit of distinction: 120 decibels
- Noise of a cymbal at 2 metres: 130 decibels
- Endurance threshold: 140 decibels
- Fighter aircraft: 150 decibels
- Rocket: 200 decibels
- Gunshot: 220 decibels

THE WORKSTATION

The workstation must be as comfortable and attractive as possible. Given that you may spend a minimum of eight hours a day there over a number of years, it is essential that you feel good about it. It is inevitable that it will have an effect on your morale, your enthusiasm for work and your creativity.

Do not hesitate to give it a personal touch! If you telework, you have complete room to manoeuvre. If you work for an employer, you will inevitably be dependent on an existing work plan and especially on a budget ...

Do not be afraid to brighten up your work space. Be innovative! If the surroundings are gloomy, do not hesitate to improve depressing working conditions for you and your colleagues.

Here are just a few suggestions:

- Repaint the walls.
- Change the type of lamp (choose halogen lamps ahead of neon ones).
- Buy some plants.
- Install some brightly coloured Venetian blinds.
- Decorate your office with paintings or familiar objects.
- Add a few (preferably colourful) personal touches.

Posture

The posture chosen for working is fundamental. Sustained stress on the vertebral column in a poor position may cause fatigue and, of course, in the long term, painful and sometimes permanent backaches. The first rule is therefore to find a table/seat/body/hand relationship which allows you to comfortably work for a long time.

The work surface

The work surface must be functional, practical and in no way cluttered with objects liable to slow you down.

Figure 10.2: The ideal position – at right-angles to the screen

- The height of the surface on which the screen and computer rest must be 65 to 75 cm. For small people, a footrest is essential.

- The horizontal area of the work surface must be at least 80 by 120 cm.

- The depth for the knees and legs should usually be 90 cm so that they do not hit the uprights of the work surface.

The screen

- The position of the display screen in terms of the distance from your eyes must be between 50 cm and 70 cm.

- The slope of the front of the screen must be between 15° and 20°.

- The user must be able to pivot and rotate in order to avoid reflections, for example.

▬▬▬ The seat

The seat must be chosen with regard to your:

- lumbar curves (back shape)
- arteriovenous circulation (blood circulation)
- musculotendinous physiology (body shape and size).

It must be fitted with castors if you have cause to pivot frequently.

It may be fitted with armrests, but these must not under any circumstances hinder the mobility of the arms and hands.

 Symptoms such as aches in the back, neck, shoulders, arms and wrists may entail curvature of the vertebral column, muscular pains, varicose veins, chronic fatigue and headaches. The symptoms are warning signals, do not take them lightly!

Figure 10.3: Your day-to-day work corner

THE KEYBOARD

The ergonomic keyboard reduces the curvature of the wrist during typing to a minimum (see Hour 3).

THE TEN COMMANDMENTS

- The level of the eyes must be located on average 1.15 m from the ground, with a standard seat height of 40 to 45 cm.

- The keyboard must be 70 or 80 cm above the ground.

- The seat back must be adjustable to match the best lumbar posture for each person.

- The height of the seat must be adjustable.

- The seat must pivot and be fitted with castors if movements and rotations are frequent and necessary.

- The seat must not have armrests that hinder the mobility of the arms.

- There must be a footrest for small people.

- The height between the seat and the table must be between 20 and 30 cm so that there is sufficient room for the knees.

- The screen must be at right-angles to the plane of vision.

- The user must have a copyholder, located 70 cm from the screen, if inputting is the main activity of his job.

Workstation ergonomics is therefore to be taken seriously. It has an effect on both the quality of your work and your psychological well-being. Do not add stress to stress! Professional life is often quite difficult enough. Make sure that your working environment is as pleasant as possible in order to spare you unnecessary pain and upset, anxiety, chronic fatigue, appetite problems and, of course, aggressiveness!

Conquering the working environment is very often the result of conquering yourself. Create a pleasant and comfortable environment and you will find that you become more motivated in your work.

TELEWORKING

Your computer need not only be for leisure and games – you can also use it to earn a living. Along with a printer, fax machine, telephone, modem and Internet connection, you can use your PC to conduct business at local, regional or global level from the comfort of your own home.

Advantages of teleworking

- **Freedom**: teleworking allows you to be your own boss, with no more duties to perform other than your own. You no longer need work in difficult surroundings and circumstances. Rather, you are free to do whatever you want.

- **No more travelling**: the time spent commuting to and from the workplace is on average approximately three hours per employee. In recent years, this time has increased greatly in urban areas. Not only does travelling waste a lot of our time every day, but it generates significant fatigue and not inconsiderable hearing stress.

- **Savings**: teleworking also allows you to save money on travelling expenses and clothes.

- **A tailor-made job**: because you have chosen to work for yourself, there is no conflict between what you consider should be done and what you actually do.

- **Job creation**: in developing your own work situation, you are bound to have opened one or more markets. These opportunities are beneficial not only to you but may also benefit others. In the course of time, you may – if your business goes well – become an employer yourself.

Drawbacks of teleworking

- **Freedom**: some people attracted by the prospect of teleworking – or sometimes compelled to do so – may quickly become disillusioned. Remember that teleworking is not for everyone. Some people feel reassured by the presence of an employer, a structured organisation and the regularity of pay slips. Confronted with complete freedom, they may very well slip into bad habits and laziness.

- **Lack of stress**: many of us function on "surges of adrenalin" and stress. But when you are working on your own at home, how do you generate this atmosphere of stress and competition that is the great attraction of office life and without which work would be so dull? Stress is an essential regulator of tension. How do you recover from tension when you are alone facing your computer screen? The first source of stress is, of course, the rent to be paid and the invoices of all kinds. The second source of stress results quite simply from the urgent jobs and assignments you agree to take on.

- **The psychological aspect**: some people are terrified of solitude. They have a vital need for conversation and contact, and adapt very badly to working on their own. Before starting to work from home, you must make sure that you have the right temperament.

- **Working 24 hours a day**: when you start up, it is tempting to work 24 hours a day, sacrificing quality of life, well-being and contact with your family. Remember that no-one is safe from depression related to tedious and unenjoyable excess work. Take regular breaks, exercise or even go on holiday. You might even consider taking a nap in the middle of the day – it is better to work efficiently for two or three hours than to work unproductively for seven or eight hours without a break.

Figure 10.4: To telework or not to telework?

TELEWORKING OCCUPATIONS

- **Writer**: the main quality required of an author is relative independence of mind and a certain creativity in order to be in a position to design and submit projects. You also need to be tenacious, good at forming relationships, persuasive and patient.

- **Freelance journalist**: if you are looking to earn lots of money, it is better to forget freelance journalism. The only items which work and pay reasonably well concern high technologies and the Internet; otherwise the money is not particularly good. Few freelance journalists manage to earn a reasonable living. Those who do are usually involved in other activities. Only choose freelance journalism if you are prepared to work initially to merely establish a reputation.

No more traffic jams!

Figure 10.5: Teleworking means you no longer have to travel

- **Computer consultant**: this may work out well quite quickly. Computer service companies use the services of independent consultants, which spares them from having to pay employees. Depending on your abilities, you can easily ask for between £150 to £200 per day.

- **Graphic designer or illustrator**: publicity and communication agencies may call upon your talents as a graphic designer for publicity or commercial brochures. With a little luck, you may even get into newspaper publishing and become a cartoonist. This would of course require you to have expertise in XPress, Illustrator and Photoshop plus access to a colour laser printer.

- **Secretary**: the time devoted to canvassing is one of the keys to business success. In addition to perfectly mastering current electronic office tools, a secretary must therefore be excellent at marketing. Secretaries carry out tasks such as book-keeping and administrative work for small companies, but tend not to be involved in inputting work. If you want to become a secretary, remember that the market has a tendency to be overcrowded.

- **Trainer**: trainers provide instruction in the Internet and office software programs. They also act as on-call computer consultants, sometimes working from home and sometimes working at the premises of the training organisation.

- **And the others ...** engineers, remote maintenance technicians, draughtsmen, translators, proofreaders, marketing people, etc.

By the year 2000, Europe will have around 10 million teleworkers.

Figure 10.6: What type of teleworker are you?

THE STATUS OF THE TELEWORKER

Labour regulations specify clearly that someone who works from home is an employee. Nevertheless, 9 out of 10 people who carry out an activity from home have the status of a self-employed person or have created their own company.

- **Employee**: to enjoy employee status, you must first of all work for one or more employers who provide you with regular or intermittent work.

As evidence of your employee status, you will get:

- either a signed contract specifying the collective agreement to which your employer is bound,
- or pay slips.

You, of course, enjoy all the advantages of employee status, including paid holidays, Social Security and unemployment benefit.

As regards earnings, you may be paid by the hour, by the day, or by the task.

- **Self-employed person**: the self-employed person has no hierarchical connection with an employer. He or she is his or her own boss. He or she can practise a profession, be a craftsman, a tradesman or a sales representative, for example.

  If you sell a product, you are a tradesman. If you produce, repair or convert, you are a craftsman. If you practise an intellectual activity, you practise a profession (for example: author, freelance journalist, computer consultant, etc.). Half the people practising a professional activity choose the form of **sole trader**, since this requires no initial capital. You need to fill in a self-employed business declaration. You will also need to keep your own accounts and fill in your own tax returns. However, you can reclaim tax on expenses connected with your business, for example purchasing your computer, business phone calls and travel expenses. For more detailed information you should contact your local tax office.

- **Business company creator**: this has the advantage that you do not need to offer your own property as collateral for any company debts, but has the disadvantage that initial capital is required.

- **Limited liability company**: requires a start-up capital of £5,000, with a minimum of two partners. If you are a minority partner, you benefit from the tax system for employees. If you are a majority partner, the profits from your company will be integrated with your tax on the income.

- **Private limited company under sole ownership**: requires a start-up capital of £5,000 and a minimum of one single person.

Many people, particularly the under-forties, would like to try teleworking, since it offers them the chance to better manage their time.

THE DIFFERENT FORMS OF TELEWORKING

There are different forms of teleworking. These can take the following different forms according to the individual, the socio-economic context and the catchment area:

- **Working from home**: a subject enlarged upon earlier.

- **Mobile teleworking**: mainly used by sales representatives equipped with their mobile phone and by sales engineers who are nevertheless attached to a fixed base.

- **Part-time telework and telecommuting**: an employee carries out certain tasks at home using remote data transmission in order to reduce the time wasted due to travelling.

- **Teleworking from a tele-office**: making appointments for a doctor's surgery, canvassing for a business firm, etc.

- **Teleworking away from the office**: employees nevertheless stay in contact with the parent company by means of remote data transmission tools.

It is obvious that one of the major ingredients for making teleworking profitable is the Internet, which allows you to draw on sources of information for hours on end – hours that you would otherwise use for travelling, thus making you more productive. A normal employee may spend 5 to 6% of his working time on learning, whereas you have 3 hours every day – from the comfort of your own home.

Hour 11

Making the right purchase

THE CONTENTS FOR THIS HOUR

- Making the right purchase
- Breaking even
- The well-known makes
- Buying over the Internet
- Buying from supermarkets
- Assembling your PC
- Promotions
- Obtaining lists of hardware and software from the Internet
- Receiving the latest software on free trial

MAKING THE RIGHT PURCHASE

Knowing what to buy and when is an art in itself. It is better to wait for the right moment rather than to rush out and buy the latest product as soon as it is released. You will find the wait is worth it when the product is upgraded. If a product is well marketed, its price invariably drops; if the number of models sold increases tenfold, the price is reduced by approximately half. For example, a CD writer cost approximately £1600 in 1995; in 1998 it cost less than £200.

BREAKING EVEN

In order to make the right purchase, you have to take into consideration what the equipment offers. "To break even" describes the point where you neither gain nor lose, the point at which income equals expenditure. For example, between 1995 and 1997 it was possible to rent CD writers for £25 per weekend, while CDs cost between £5 and £8. Obviously, as CDs now cost no more than £1 and machines no more than £200, it is better for you to buy rather than rent.

You can buy your equipment:

- from your nearest retailer, who should stock individual parts as well

- from a dealer specialising in the well-known makes

- from a supermarket

- by mail order or via the Internet

- from the second-hand market

THE WELL-KNOWN MAKES

It is obviously tempting to buy a well-known make, especially if you want to resell your hardware for a reasonable price. However, be aware that major suppliers have for some time now operated proprietary systems. This means that you often have to continue buying the same make. What happens is that particular features are artificially integrated that make the hardware incompatible and sometimes prevent the supplier's hardware from functioning properly on other configurations. In some cases, you can get round these difficulties using patches and drivers that you can find on the Internet.

Having said that, buying from a well-known supplier gives you security, as it is in the interest of the supplier to provide you with high-quality products in order to retain your custom. Excellent hardware can be purchased from either a big name or a small retailer.

BUYING OVER THE INTERNET

Buying over the Internet is very tempting and offers numerous advantages, not least the fact that products are up to 20% cheaper. Compared to shopping from catalogues, you can save up to 20% on high-quality software. For example, Meta Creation's Art Dabbler, which you could buy from a catalogue for approximately £35 in 1998, costs approximately £29 if you buy it over the Internet. If you are content to download a product (only paying the licence and not receiving the full package), you will obviously pay considerably less. You will not get an instruction manual or CD-ROM, but then the help files are often enough.

Figure 11.1: Mail-ordering – the LDLC site...

Figure 11.2: ... and the Soft Gallery logo

BUYING FROM SUPERMARKETS

It is important to pay attention to what you buy. At first sight, the prices may appear excellent, but in the end you usually get what you pay for. Specific promotions on specific items of hardware may look attractive, but complete configurations do not always contain parts that are standard across the board. You may not get such high-quality models as you would from a local dealer. For example, you may find that a computer costing approximately £750 uses different brands of memory linear array that cannot function together. So although you may get a scanner and printer thrown in for free, you will probably have to take the computer back to the shop two or three times before the whole thing works – assuming the shop is able to remedy the problem.

The main problem with buying from supermarkets is that, in order to attract customers, they sell their computers at almost cost price and that suppliers' prices are very low. This means that the computers sold may not be so easily upgraded.

ASSEMBLING YOUR PC

The best way of purchasing a PC is to specify or construct it yourself, which allows you to carefully choose each individual component you install and therefore to customise the computer to your needs.

If you choose to assemble your PC yourself, you will probably want an application that includes the following applications:

- graphics

- word-processing

- games.

For each of these applications, you can choose from various options.

Using your PC for graphics applications

Choosing a Pentium II motherboard with an Ultra-Wide SCSI controller in order to use a hard disk of this type allows you to work faster when using Windows to run software programs such as Adobe Photoshop, Painter, 3D Studio MAX and other memory-intensive software applications. The speed of the hard disk will enable you to work faster. You will also find it easier to add numerous peripherals. These will need 64 Mb or more of SDRAM.

Pentium II motherboards have an in-built AGP video bus. An AGP video card can also be used by people with cable television. In all cases, it is best to go for a digital format if you want to rapidly switch from your TV to your computer.

Finally, a 20" or 21" 1200 × 1600 screen is the ultimate in luxury. You can buy one for less than £900 with an on-site three-year guarantee. Having said that, a 17" screen is just as good once the settings have been changed to 1,024 × 768.

Using your PC for word-processing applications

Word-processing applications do not place major requirements on the configuration. A Pentium with 32 Mb of RAM will do fine. To comfortably handle most tasks, you will need a 4 Mb graphics card and 17" screen.

Using your PC for playing games

Today's games require power, memory and preferably a 3D graphics card. This takes the strain off the processor and cuts down on the time you have to wait. If you can, choose a Pentium II motherboard, a minimum 233 Mhz Pentium II Intel processor and 32 Mb of SDRAM.

PROMOTIONS

These never last long and are intended to attract and keep customers. They concern pretty much all kinds of equipment: screens, memory and peripherals. Although computer magazines are a good source of up-to-date information, many dealers advertise their promotions in fliers which you can only obtain from their store. Prices change so quickly that updates sometimes appear every week.

Remember that promotions only run while stocks last. You will also find promotions on various Internet sites.

Obtaining lists of hardware and software from the Internet

A good way of keeping informed is to consult lists available on the Internet. These deal mostly with configuration problems or questions regarding what equipment to buy. These issues are well discussed and will help you solve your problem or make your decision. For example, if you want to buy a CD writer, consulting these lists may help you avoid making the wrong purchase.

Some lists also offer links related to a particular subject. For example, if you want to buy a 3DFX graphics card, people who have the same card may be able to point you in the direction of other sites exclusively dedicated to this card. You may, for example, have problems installing a new hard disk or AGP card. If you do, just connect to the mailing list address, describe your problem and you may be lucky enough to get a reply from someone who has experienced exactly the same problem and can offer a solution. It may be you will have to buy a new product, which, as we have seen earlier, can also be done over the Internet.

You may have to wait a few hours for a reply – but then again you may get one in a matter of minutes. It is this instantaneousness of information that is the main advantage of the Internet. All you need to do is to be able to navigate around it properly.

RECEIVING THE LATEST SOFTWARE ON FREE TRIAL

You can also subscribe to mailing lists from which you can obtain advice on downloading the latest software on free trial. Each day, you will find twenty or so new products accompanied by a description and their file size.

Hour 12

The future

THE CONTENTS FOR THIS HOUR

- Becoming an advanced user
- No time to read the instructions?
- Forums and lists
- Courses
- Learning to program

BECOMING AN ADVANCED USER

Approximately 80% of users use less than 20% of the features of their programs. This is especially true of Excel, but it is also true of word-processing programs such as Word. There are at least two reasons for this:

- the instructions are dense and often difficult to understand
- different people have different needs and it is not necessary to know everything.

Having said that, you will still find people using text columns without section breaks, with the result that they do not know how to work with newspaper columns.

There are three ways of becoming an advanced user:

- Reading a little bit of the instructions every day
- Registering with Internet forums or mailing lists
- Following a course.

NO TIME TO READ THE INSTRUCTIONS?

You will probably have to buy one or two dedicated instruction manuals in order to use your software. Some of them are small and practical, while others are so large that you might want to have them as reference but are rarely likely to consult them. If you feel you just do not have the time at work, try reading small sections while in the bath, on the bus or train, or in a waiting room.

FORUMS AND LISTS

The Internet and its forums can provide you with a wealth of information. All you need is some knowledge of online communication and you can obtain information on almost anything you want – sometimes without knowing it.

COURSES

A good way of learning is to follow a course. Some companies will contribute a certain amount of money towards having their employees trained in IT, since it is the company that ultimately benefits. However, even if yours does not, it is always worth following a course, as your newly acquired skills could help you in your career (particularly if you wish to train as a software or hardware engineer, for which there is always a demand). Courses may last from one to three days right up to three to nine months.

There are also "universities" on the Internet which provide distance learning courses. You can even get a diploma – usually by paying a certain amount of money. Basically, there will always be a way for anyone who wants to learn IT to do so.

LEARNING TO PROGRAM

Few activities offer as many options as programming. Not only is there the satisfaction of creating your own software program; there is also the challenge of mastering the difficult syntax and logic of the computer. However, you will find that the hard work pays off. Learning to program is probably one of the best investments you can make as the owner of a PC. All you have to do is choose a language.

▅▅▅ Visual Basic (Microsoft)

For fans of Microsoft, Visual Basic constitutes the best choice, even if the language was initially a bit heavy and limited. It is probably still a bit too heavy, particularly because you have to add a few error management lines to each module and cannot add them globally to the application that is running. However, Visual Basic has improved with each new version. It is not as 'object oriented' as one might wish, and, up until version five at least, you had to use another language to create objects to put in the library with a view to using them later.

Nevertheless, Visual Basic has made good progress, with each new version containing a large chunk of what the previous version lacked. The visual and graphic aspect of the language makes it easy to work with, while the Internet and most dealers have large libraries full of additions in the form of OCX or ActiveX objects.

▅▅▅ Delphi and Pascal (Inprise, e.g. Borland)

Pascal is a language, whereas Delphi is a language that at the same offers a complete environment that is almost an operating system (one level up from an application system, at any rate).

Delphi and Pascal are structured languages that derive their popularity from the power that their structure offers. Although they have their devoted fans, their syntax is a little heavy, with the systematic use of conventional symbols restricting the modules somewhat. A major advantage of Delphi is that it allows you to create objects directly and put them in the library for later use.

You can download a trial version of Delphi from the following address:

http://www.inprise.com/download.html

Other languages

You can also choose from the following languages:

- C
- C + +
- Assembler
- SmallTalk
- Eiffel

All these languages are used in the workplace. They may initially be more difficult to learn than those previously mentioned and are not always particularly powerful. They are usually taught at university or college and are not well suited to self-instruction.

Glossary

A

@: The @ sign is one of the constituent elements of the electronic address. Since a person always has an address at an access provider, the name of the latter always appears after the @ sign. For example: Lulu@sdv.co.uk. In plain language, Lulu has an address at the access provider "sdv" located in the UK, abbreviated to "uk", where "co" indicates a company.

Access provider: The service provider who offers an Internet connection to its subscribers.

Access time: The time which a disk drive, floppy disk drive or CD-ROM drive requires to find information.

Address: Location of data on the hard disk or on the diskette.

Alta Vista: One of the most efficient search engines on the Net.

Application: Synonym for a software program whose aim is to implement certain specific computing tasks such as word-processing or mathematical operations. The word-processor and the spreadsheet are two applications.

B

Backup: Action of making a copy of a document on a diskette.

Bandwidth: Maximum amount of data measured in bits per second (bps). The bandwidth can be compared to the width of a motorway. According to whether there are 2 to 8 lanes available on each side, the amount of traffic allowed under good conditions will vary enormously. The bandwidth defines the number of users and amount of traffic which a server can reasonably handle. There is a conflict of interest between the desire of the access provider to acquire the maximum number of clients while investing as little as possible, and that of the client who hopes to pay a minimum amount for a quality service. In order to make the most of the bandwidth, the modems must be as fast as possible.

BIOS: Abbreviation of *Basic Input Output System*. The BIOS adapts an operating system to its hardware environment.

Bit: Contraction of *Binary Digit*. Information element with a value of zero or one.

1 byte = 8 bits.

BPS: Bits per second; unit of measurement for the data transmission speed.

Browser: Navigator which makes it possible to gain access to information on the Web.

Buffer: Buffer memory used as a temporary storage area. Printers have their own buffer.

Bug: Error in a software program.

Bus: Set of cables and communication channels which transfer the information inside the computer.

Byte: 8 bits.

C

Cache: Intermediate memory intended to store the most recently used information.

CAD: Computer aided design. Used for production and wherever there is industrial design.

Capacity: Amount of data which can be stored on a disk. The unit of measurement is the byte, divided into kilobytes, Megabytes or Gigabytes.

CD-ROM: *Compact Disc Read-Only Memory*. This collects together text, images and sound, which may be read from a CD-ROM drive installed on a computer.

Chip: Integrated circuit.

Client: A computer which requests data from the server computer.

Client/server architecture: Combination of the following three elements:
Server computer / Client computer / Network.

Clip-art: Drawings on computer supplied in library form and classified by subject.

Compatibility: Ability of a computer to run software produced for another computer.

Computer: Machine that automates the processing of information. The first computer was the ENIAC, the most user-friendly is the Macintosh, the most widespread is the IBM PC. It has a strong position on the market and has become indispensable to the majority of people.

Computer language: Code made up of a syntax and a grammar making it possible to program. The efficiency of a language stems from its simplicity, the richness of its vocabulary and the way in which it is structured. Amongst the best-known languages are Cobol, C++, Fortran, Java, Pascal and Visual Basic.

CPU: Central microprocessor.

Cracker: Computer specialist who resolves problems, as opposed to a hacker, who creates them.

Cyber: The cyber culture is made up of everything to do with the new communication technologies and the modes of thought they generate. Comes from the Greek *cyber,* which means to steer.

Cybercafé: Café in which it is possible to have a drink while being able to access the Internet. The cost of access is around £3 for half an hour.

D

Dedicated: A software program entirely dedicated to, for example, graphics design.

Density: Amount of data which a diskette may contain. There are double density diskettes (360 kb to 720 kb) and high density diskettes (1.44 Mb to 2.8 Mb).

Digital: The opposite of analogue. A system used by computers to analyse data, whereby 0 signifies off and 1 signifies on.

Dongle: Electronic key which plugs into a port and makes it possible to protect a software program against piracy.

DOS: Disk operating system. DOS is one of the most widespread operating systems.

Dpi: Dots per inch, the unit for measuring resolution.

Driver: Small program which provides the transfer of data between two items of hardware which are not compatible. For example, a printer is delivered with a driver which translates its compatibilities.

DVD-ROM: the successor of the CD-ROM whose data storage capacity is 4 to 16 Gbytes.

E

Electronic address: Personal address for receiving electronic mail on the Internet. Not to be confused with the URL, the Internet address for a site.

Electronic mail (*e-mail*): Mail exchanged between two computers.

E-mail: Electronic mail.

Ergonomics: Technique which concerns the adaptation of work to man in the most user-friendly and comfortable way possible.

Eudora: Software which manages electronic mail.

F

FAQ (*Frequently Asked Question*): Questions very often asked concerning a particular computing field. On the Internet, each newsgroup contains an FAQ column, which is intended to reply to the most common questions asked by users.

FAT (*File Allocation Table*): Table created by disks in order to be able to pinpoint the location of files.

File Transfer Protocol (FTP): Protocol for transferring files on the Internet.

Formatting: Technique which prepares the disk or diskette for receiving computer data.

Four-colour printing: cyan, magenta, yellow and black make up the set of subtractive colours.

Freeware: System for distributing free software, written for glory alone and often excellent. Spreadsheets, word-processors and management programs flourish in this form. Not to be confused with *Shareware*.

G

GIF: *Graphic Image File Format*: The most widespread compressed graphics format of the Internet.

Graphics accelerator: Screen card which makes it possible to accelerate the processing speed of information to be displayed.

H

Hard disk: System composed of a mechanism and a rigid disk situated inside the central unit. The hard disk is used to store millions, perhaps even thousands of millions, of bytes.

Hardware: Computer hardware: case, keyboard, screen, central unit and peripherals. The opposite of software.

Home page: On the Internet, the welcome page or first page of a site.

Hot line: Telephone assistance concerning both the software and the computer hardware.

Hypertext: Technique which allows you to create links between documents of different types. Multimedia and its CD-ROM applications promote the creation of hypertext links and make navigation from term to term and from concept to concept much richer and much faster.

Hypertext link: Link between information from document to document. Allows information to be accessed extremely quickly.

I

Infoway: Information highway. International transfer of information by cable.

Infopoor/inforich: Expression designating the gulf which is widening between the companies and countries with access to computing, to the information highways, to communication in general, and those which do not. Is the Internet going to increase the difference or promote equality of opportunity?

Integrated: Said of a software package which contains all of the following: a spreadsheet, word processor, database, and perhaps even a graphics program.

Interface: The interface connects the user to the software and to the hardware environment of his computer. It should be user-friendly and pleasant to use. Windows is considered to be a user-friendly interface since graphics with icons is a highly intuitive method of access.

Internaut: An Internet fanatic whose daily presence on the Net is 14 hours a day on average!

Internet: Also called the World Wide Web, to date the Internet makes it possible to connect around 30 million users who exchange electronic mail, information, and participate in discussion groups. Often abbreviated to the Net.

Internet Explorer: Name of the Microsoft program for navigating on the Net. It competes with Netscape Navigator created by the company Netscape.

Intranet: The Intranet is a local network as opposed to the Internet, which is a worldwide network. The Intranet may possibly have the same technical characteristics as the Internet: the same programs and the same protocols.

J

Java: Language developed by Sun Microsystems, used for programming on the Net. It was created by James Gosling.

Joystick: Lever connected to the computer like all peripherals and allowing very quick movements on the screen. The joystick is used for games software.

JPEG: *Joint Photographic Expert Group*: The data compression standard for fixed images. Graphics file format widely used on the Internet.

K

Key: Keyboard key.

L

Laser: *Light Amplification by Stimulated Emission of Radiation*: Technique using a beam of light to perform various tasks.

Local network: Group of computers connected by cable in the same office or the same company.

M

Macintosh: Created in 1984, the Macintosh succeeded the Apple II.

Maintenance: Function which makes it possible to keep both the software and hardware of the computer in good working order.

Megabyte: 1,048,576 bytes.

Modem: Modulator/demodulator. A microprocessor peripheral enabling the PC to communicate with other computers via a telephone line and to connect to the Internet network.

Multimedia: Simultaneous use of text, sound, image and video within the same application.

Multitasking: Quality of the operating system allowing it to run several applications at the same time. Windows is a multitasking operating system.

N

Nano: Prefix signifying one thousand-millionth.

Netscape Navigator: Name of the Netscape program for navigating on the Net. It competes with Microsoft's Internet Explorer.

Network: System for communicating between computers connected to one another by cable. The aim is to facilitate the exchange of data and to promote co-operation in work and skills.

Notebook: Small lightweight portable computer (3 to 6 kilos).

Notepad: Diary provided with software which allows you to manage appointments.

Novell: Company which specialises in network management.

O

Offline: Said of a peripheral which is disconnected or put on standby. Also an electronic product such as a diskette or CD-ROM which does not require any connection.

Online: Said of a computer when it is switched on. Also characterises the exchange of data from computer to computer.

Optical fibre: Cable made of a transparent material by means of which the information flows in the form of light. At the start, it is coded by a laser. On arrival, it is decoded by a diode. It is instantaneous and totally reliable.

OS/2: Operating system created by IBM for PCs.

P

Package: Group of several software programs in the same sales promotion. By extension, the packaging of the software or CD-ROM.

Parallel port: Port situated on the central unit and which is used for connecting printers.

Path: Path for accessing data on the hard disk.

PC: *Personal Computer*.

Pentium: Name of the Intel 80586 microprocessor.

Pictogram: Icon.

Pitch: Distance which separates two pixels on a screen.

Port: Connector situated on the external face of the computer which makes it possible to connect the motherboard situated in the central unit to the peripherals. The majority of computers are equipped with at least one serial port and one parallel port.

Portable: Small travelling computer which works on batteries. From the heavy transportable to the lightweight *notebook*, a wide range is available.

Program Manager: Part of the Windows 3 graphical interface which allows programs to be run.

Q

QWERTY: Name given to the American keyboard which derives from the first line of keys.

R

Rack: Case which packages software or CD-ROMs, provided with a hole which allows it to be threaded on a metal rod.

RAM (*Random Access Memory*): Computer memory which can be read and written.

Reverse video: Reversal of the writing and the background.

Root: Initial directory of the hard disk or diskette.

S

Scanner: Device which allows you to enter photographic or text documents into the computer. The operation is the same as that of the photocopier.

Search engine: Program for searching on the Internet according to key words entered by the user. It may be compared to the index of a book: the Internet is a giant book of several thousand million pages and the key words make it possible to quickly access relevant specialised information. The main search engines are offered as free services. They periodically run through the whole complex: the sites, newsgroups and FTPs. In this way, destroyed or modified links are removed from the database or updated.

Serial port: Port situated on the central unit and which is used for connecting serial peripherals (modems, printers, etc.).

Server: Central computer offering its services on a network.

Shareware: Software protected by copyright, part of which you can try out on trial and pay for if satisfied with it.

Silicon Valley: A famous valley situated near San Francisco (California) where many companies responsible for the development of computing have been established.

Single sheet: Method of inserting sheets into the printer.

Site: Location on the Internet consisting of a welcome page and various other pages, the aim of which is to present a work, an idea, or simply act as an introduction using multimedia tools such as sound, text, image. There are millions of sites on the Internet.

Site extractor: a program which copies a complete site from the server to the user's hard disk. The importance of this is to allow offline perusal. For example, you can download at night for 50p per hour on the Internet and look at it during the day free of charge instead of paying £1.50 per hour (the cost of looking at it online).

Snail: Name given to the normal mail service because of its slowness compared with electronic mail.

Software: Program.

Splash window: Waiting window intended to help the computer user to be patient when an application takes a long time to start up. The splash window indicates the origin of the program, the name of the designer, etc.

Spreadsheet: Software which is used to perform operations with figures and tables. The most famous spreadsheet is Microsoft Excel.

Station-to-station network: Group of computers, each of which can act as both client and server.

Surfer: The Internet user who goes from site to site.

SuperVGA (SVGA): High-quality screen card.

Switch: Device which makes it possible to change from one printer to another.

System diskette: Diskette whose function is to start up the computer.

T

TCP/IP (*Transmission Control Protocol/Internet Protocol*): Protocol for transmitting files on the Internet, co-invented by Vinton Cerf.

Teleworking: Working from home carried out on a computer via the Internet. This solution grants you freedom of action to go beyond the constraints of your work catchment area. Teleworking can be very efficient if the status of the teleworker is clearly established at the beginning.

Tree-structure: Structure of the directories on your disk.

U

Uninterruptible power supply: Device which protects computers from power failures.

Unix: Operating system written in the C language.

URL (*Uniform Resource Locator*): The address of a site on the Internet. For example: http://www.yahoo.com.

Usenet: Newsgroup network on the Internet.

V

VGA: The PC display standard. Its definition is 640 × 480.

Virtual: In the computing field, the term *virtual universe* is used to describe a structure in which all the parameters can be offered in a variety of forms and updated. In today's language, this term is the opposite of *real*.

Virus: Program which hackers devise to destroy other programs or files.

W

Warm start: Starting up the computer without turning off the power.

Webmaster: On the Internet, the master of the web. This person is responsible for managing a server or a discussion forum.

Wide area network: Group of computers geographically very far apart and connected by cable.

Windows: User-friendly graphical interface created by Microsoft.

Winsock: Set of standards intended for programs running on the Internet.

Word-processor: Software which is used to process text and all kinds of written documents. The most famous is Microsoft Word.

Worldwide network: The Internet.

World Wide Wait: Nickname given to the Internet when data transfers take too long.

World Wide Web: The interface for navigation on the Internet. Its abbreviation is WWW or Web.

X

XLS: Extension for Excel spreadsheet files.

XPress: Desktop publishing software designed for the Macintosh and published by Quark Corporation.

Y

Yahoo!: American search engine on the Internet.

Z

Zip: File compression format. The expression "zipping a file" is used.

Zoom: Function allowing the magnification of an image represented under Windows.

Index